GREAT MOVIE
MISTAKES 3

Jon Sandys

THANKS

Thanks to Super Grover, amycamille1975, Hamster, THGhost, Mortug, Brad, wizard_of_gore, manthabeat, Quantom X, André VinÃcius, jbrbbt, GalahadFairlight, AD, Friso94, johnrosa, Jazetopher, LizzieWD, Ssiscool, NancyFelix, kmbly@radford.edu, ????, dishmanchicago, kh1616, korporal kool, troy fox, Movie_Freak 1, Necrothesp, Sentinel, William Bergquist, Aaron Chi Thomas, jerimiah, paolog, Len Mulaski, Robert F Baptista, Scott215, padfootrocksmysocks, StevenJ, Aerinah, fishbiscuits, turkman143, Amitai Assido, Disney-Freak, Twotall, Phixius, mightymick, JamesP, imshiffman, James Kennedy, Dr Wilson, Drpd21, DavidK93, goofyfoot, Jennifer 1, Christie_Love, nerac, trina, Heather Benton, James King III, Jack Vaughan, majorlagg, Charles Austin Miller, Stan McCulloch, mdlovin, The Nachoman, Anthorin, igzz, ajp, Regulus, abathgate, Arjak, Tobias Straka, Phaneron, Matdan97, Ryanpowell, paankracyk, freedom2006, Pier Pistocchi, Guy, Cubs Fan, Jacob La Cour, Sacha, Bishop73, ACertainShadeofGreen, James T Hampton Jr., BarrysBaby, poehitman, nightline, Vader47000, Darren Manick, OneHappyHusky, Grumpy Scot, Blue321, Lummie, CC, Igor Babichev, Our_Man_Flint, polaris, ckstaats, and all the anonymous submitters who helped make this book, and moviemistakes.com, what they are.

Thank you for buying this book! I hope you enjoy it, and if so please tell your friends, share it, lend it...spread the word! I'd love to hear any suggestions, corrections, thoughts and opinions - please get in touch at jon@moviemistakes.com. And please leave a review on Amazon - if you like this, there's plenty more where this came from. And if you've got any observations of your own, please submit them to moviemistakes.com and let other people know about them!

Text © Jon Sandys 1996-2019

Images © their respective creators/owners, credited under each image.

The images reproduced here are done so for the purpose of commentary and criticism, and are a small, low-resolution part of the work they relate to.

ABOUT THE SITE
AND THE AUTHOR

I cannot lie - I haven't spotted all of these myself. After all, I've only got one pair of eyes, and only one lifetime! They've been accumulated over the past 20 years from myself and thousands of other eagle-eyed fans across the world, and all stored on my website, moviemistakes.com. But rather than forcing you to trawl through the 100,000+ entries on the site, I thought it was worth selecting the cream of the crop for a book like this.

Back in September 1996, I was 17 years old, a huge film fan, and fairly computer obsessed. I wanted to make a web page, but couldn't really think of what to do. I eventually took a few continuity mistakes and film facts, put them into a website along with an e-mail address, and that was about it. Over time, thanks to word of mouth and the occasional bit of press, it's built into the collection it is today, covering TV shows, even books and games, and including trivia, quotes and more.

This book is primarily designed to point you in the direction of all those little things in TV shows that you may not have noticed the first, or second, or even third time around. It is for entertainment and educational purposes only. It should not prevent you from going go on with your life as normal. I take no responsibility when you're next watching something and catch yourself thinking 'I'm sure her sleeves were rolled up in the last shot...' But, if after reading it, you no longer can watch things without picking them apart for the most minute mistakes, I'm afraid there's only one piece of advice I can give you...you'll always find a home with similarly afflicted people at moviemis-takes.com.

A NOTE ABOUT TIMES

Lots of the entries here have times after them, when the mistake happens. Due to the nature of different releases, and especially the difference between formats, the times might be approximate. For example NTSC (used in the US) and PAL (used in lots of other places) mean times can be off by 4% (to do with frame rates - I won't bore you with the technical side here, but Google will help you out if you're keen!). So if you're trying to find something and the time doesn't seem right, go forwards/back a bit and you should find the relevant scene.

CONTENTS

Moana (2016)
The Mummy Returns (2001)
Planes, Trains & Automobiles (1987)
Pretty Woman (1990)
Prince of Persia: The Sands of Time (2010)
Red Dragon (2002)
Shallow Hal (2001)
The Simpsons Movie (2007)
Star Wars (1977)
Star Wars: The Force Awakens (2015)
The Sum of All Fears (2002)
To All the Boys I've Loved Before (2018)
Top Gun (1986)
Training Day (2001)
Transformers: Revenge of the Fallen (2009)
The Transporter (2002)
Twister (1996)
The Untouchables (1987)
The Wolverine (2013)
X-Men 3 (2006)

Visible crew/equipment

Abbott and Costello meet Frankenstein (1948)
American Psycho (2000)
Armour of God (1986)
Back to the Future (1985)
Braveheart (1995)
Casino Royale (2006)
Charlie's Angels (2000)
Cheaper by the Dozen (2003)
The Descent (2005)
E.T. the Extra-Terrestrial (1982)
The Equalizer 2 (2018)
Eyes Wide Shut (1999)
Face/Off (1997)
Ferris Bueller's Day Off (1986)
A Fish Called Wanda (1988)
Friday the 13th Part 3: 3D (1982)
Harry Potter and the Philosopher's Stone (2001)
Hellraiser (1987)
Highlander (1986)
The Hills Have Eyes 2 (2007)

The Hurt Locker (2008)
Independence Day (1996)
Indiana Jones and the Temple of Doom (1984)
Iron Man (2008)
Irreversible (2002)
Jason Bourne (2016)
Jaws (1975)
Jurassic Park III (2001)
King Kong (2005)
Labyrinth (1986)
The Lord of the Rings: The Fellowship of the Ring (2001)
The Lord of the Rings: The Return of the King (2003)
Mad Max 2 (1981)
Meet the Fockers (2004)
Minority Report (2002)
The Outsiders (1983)
Papillon (1973)
Pearl Harbor (2001)
The Ring (2002)
The Rocky Horror Picture Show (1975)
Rocky III (1982)
Rush Hour 2 (2001)
Saw 3D (2010)
Saw V (2008)
Speed (1994)
Spider-Man 2 (2004)
Split (2016)
Star Wars (1977)
Stargate (1994)
Top Gun (1986)
Troy (2004)
Factual errors
2010 (1984)
Along Came a Spider (2001)
Armageddon (1998)
Body Heat (1981)
Bohemian Rhapsody (2018)
Broken Arrow (1996)
Casino Royale (2006)
Catch Me If You Can (2002)
The Core (2003)

Dead Poets Society (1989)
Die Another Day (2002)
Django Unchained (2012)
Dunkirk (2017)
Elektra (2005)
First Man (2018)
Furious 7 (2015)
Girl, Interrupted (1999)
Gladiator (2000)
Gravity (2013)
Green Berets (1968)
Green Book (2018)
Hallowed Ground (2007)
Halloween (2007)
Halloween: The Curse of Michael Myers (1995)
High Noon (1952)
Hollow Man (2000)
The Hurt Locker (2008)
Indiana Jones and the Kingdom of the Crystal Skull (2008)
It (2017)
Joe Kidd (1972)
Kingsman: The Secret Service (2014)
Left Behind (2014)
Mission: Impossible (1996)
Murder on the Orient Express (2017)
The Outsider (2018)
Pain & Gain (2013)
The Peacemaker (1997)
Pink Floyd The Wall (1982)
Pokemon 3: The Movie (2000)
Red Tails (2012)
Ronin (1998)
Rush (2013)
San Andreas (2015)
The Santa Clause (1994)
The Social Network (2010)
Species (1995)
Spider-Man: Homecoming (2017)
Spy Game (2001)
Stripes (1981)
The Sum of All Fears (2002)

Time Bandits (1981)
Under Siege (1992)
Who Framed Roger Rabbit (1988)
Yes Man (2008)
Plot holes
2012 (2009)
Blue Thunder (1983)
Brave (2012)
Bring it On (2000)
Brother Bear 2 (2006)
Bumblebee (2018)
Capricorn One (1977)
Changing Lanes (2002)
Charley Varrick (1973)
Child's Play (1988)
Cliffhanger (1993)
Con Air (1997)
The Core (2003)
Days of Thunder (1990)
Die Hard 2 (1990)
The Eagle Has Landed (1976)
The Equalizer 2 (2018)
A Fish Called Wanda (1988)
The Fly (1986)
Friday the 13th Part 3: 3D (1982)
The Game (1997)
Gothika (2003)
Halloween 5 (1989)
Happy Gilmore (1996)
Home Alone 4 (2002)
Hostel (2005)
Inside Out (2015)
The Italian Job (1969)
Jaws (1975)
Jumping Jack Flash (1986)
Jurassic World: Fallen Kingdom (2018)
The Karate Kid III (1989)
Kiss the Girls (1997)
The Lady Vanishes (1938)
Live Free or Die Hard (2007)
The Lost World: Jurassic Park (1997)

Minority Report (2002)
Mission: Impossible - Ghost Protocol (2011)
National Treasure: Book of Secrets (2007)
On the Line (2001)
The Parent Trap (1998)
Poseidon (2006)
The Purge: Election Year (2016)
Raiders of the Lost Ark (1981)
Robocop 3 (1993)
Rogue One: A Star Wars Story (2016)
Shrek Forever After (2010)
Snakes on a Plane (2006)
Spy Kids 3-D: Game Over (2003)
Star Trek II: The Wrath of Khan (1982)
The Sum of All Fears (2002)
Terminator 3: Rise of the Machines (2003)
Toy Story (1995)
Ultraviolet (2006)
Urban Legend (1998)
Westworld (1973)
X-Men 2 (2003)
You Only Live Twice (1967)

Revealing mistakes
American Pie 2 (2001)
Beverly Hills Cop (1984)
Bugsy Malone (1976)
Cabin Fever (2002)
Casino Royale (2006)
Charlie's Angels (2000)
Christmas with the Kranks (2004)
Die Another Day (2002)
Dracula 2000 (2000)
The Fast and the Furious: Tokyo Drift (2006)
Freddy Vs. Jason (2003)
Frozen (2013)
Ghost (1990)
Gladiator (2000)
Glory (1989)
Halloween II (1981)
Harry Potter and the Chamber of Secrets (2002)
High School Musical (2006)

Home Alone (1990)
Hostel (2005)
Indiana Jones and The Last Crusade (1989)
Jaws (1975)
Jeepers Creepers (2001)
The League of Extraordinary Gentlemen (2003)
Legally Blonde (2001)
Liar Liar (1997)
The Lord of the Rings: The Fellowship of the Ring (2001)
The Man with the Golden Gun (1974)
The Matrix Reloaded (2003)
Men in Black (1997)
Midway (1976)
Miss Congeniality (2000)
Mission: Impossible - Rogue Nation (2015)
Moulin Rouge (2001)
The Mummy Returns (2001)
Never Been Kissed (1999)
The Parent Trap (1998)
Passenger 57 (1992)
The Princess Bride (1987)
Red 2 (2013)
The Rocky Horror Picture Show (1975)
Romeo and Juliet (1968)
Scream (1996)
Snake Eyes (1998)
Speed (1994)
Star Wars (1977)
Star Wars: Episode II - Attack of the Clones (2002)
Star Wars: Episode III - Revenge of the Sith (2005)
Thunderball (1965)
Troy (2004)
You Only Live Twice (1967)
Zulu (1964)
Audio problems
Ace Ventura: Pet Detective (1994)
Alex and Emma (2003)
Annie (1982)
Austin Powers: The Spy Who Shagged Me (1999)
The Aviator (2004)
The Borrowers (1997)

Camp Rock (2008)
Carry On Cabby (1963)
Catch Me If You Can (2002)
Con Air (1997)
The Dark Knight (2008)
Darkness Falls (2003)
Days of Thunder (1990)
Die Hard 2 (1990)
Dr. No (1962)
The Five Heartbeats (1991)
Friday the 13th (1980)
The Godfather (1972)
The Goonies (1985)
The Great Dictator (1940)
Halloween III: Season of the Witch (1982)
Hang 'Em High (1968)
Harry Potter and the Chamber of Secrets (2002)
High School Musical (2006)
High School Musical 2 (2007)
I Am Legend (2007)
I Know Who Killed Me (2007)
I Still Know What You Did Last Summer (1998)
Iron Monkey (1993)
The Island (2005)
Kingdom of Heaven (2005)
Lemony Snicket's A Series of Unfortunate Events (2004)
The Lion King II: Simba's Pride (1998)
Live and Let Die (1973)
Live Free or Die Hard (2007)
Look Who's Talking (1989)
The Lord of the Rings: The Two Towers (2002)
Mallrats (1995)
The Matrix (1999)
The Other Boleyn Girl (2008)
Pee-wee's Big Adventure (1985)
The Phantom of the Opera (2004)
The Room (2003)
Scooby-Doo and the Cyber Chase (2001)
The Score (2001)
Selena (1997)
Sky High (2005)

The Sound of Music (1965)
Speed (1994)
Spider-Man (2002)
Stand By Me (1986)
Star Wars: Episode I - The Phantom Menace (1999)
Surf's Up (2007)
Titanic (1997)
Transformers (2007)
Watchmen (2009)
Wedding Crashers (2005)
The World is Not Enough (1999)
You Only Live Twice (1967)
Character mistakes
3 Idiots (2009)
The Abyss (1989)
Ace Ventura: Pet Detective (1994)
Apocalypse Now (1979)
Awake (2007)
Back to the Future Part II (1989)
Christmas with the Kranks (2004)
Common mistakes
Creed II (2018)
Crimson Tide (1995)
Django Unchained (2012)
Fast & Furious 6 (2013)
Fast Times at Ridgemont High (1982)
Field of Dreams (1989)
Flight (2012)
Friday (1995)
Ghost Rider (2007)
Good Morning, Vietnam (1987)
The Great Debaters (2007)
Hanover Street (1979)
Harry Potter and the Philosopher's Stone (2001)
I Know Who Killed Me (2007)
In the Line of Fire (1993)
Inglourious Basterds (2009)
It's a Mad Mad Mad Mad World (1963)
Johnny English (2003)
Justice League: The Flashpoint Paradox (2013)
Law Abiding Citizen (2009)

Lethal Weapon 3 (1992)
The Lost World (1960)
Love Actually (2003)
Maximum Overdrive (1986)
Midway (1976)
Monster (2003)
National Lampoon's Christmas Vacation (1989)
National Treasure (2004)
Nativity! (2009)
No Country For Old Men (2007)
Ocean's Eleven (1960)
Oliver (1968)
The Open House (2018)
Prometheus (2012)
The Quick and The Dead (1987)
Rocky IV (1985)
See Spot Run (2001)
Sister Act (1992)
Sixteen Candles (1984)
Sky Captain and the World of Tomorrow (2004)
The Sons of Katie Elder (1965)
Star Trek: First Contact (1996)
Star Trek: Insurrection (1998)
Step Brothers (2008)
Street Fighter (1994)
Swimfan (2002)
Top Gun (1986)
The Towering Inferno (1974)
What A Girl Wants (2003)
White House Down (2013)
Wrong Turn 2: Dead End (2007)

Deliberate mistakes

3 Ninjas (1992)
Alice in Wonderland (2010)
Any Which Way You Can (1980)
Austin Powers: The Spy Who Shagged Me (1999)
A Beautiful Mind (2001)
Ben-Hur (1959)
The Big Lebowski (1998)
Cars (2006)
Chariots of Fire (1981)

Contact (1997)
Darkman (1990)
Donnie Darko (2001)
Dressed to Kill (1980)
Failure To Launch (2006)
Fled (1996)
Forrest Gump (1994)
Fury (2014)
The Game (1997)
Ghost Ship (2002)
Gladiator (2000)
Groundhog Day (1993)
Labyrinth (1986)
The Lion King (1994)
Live and Let Die (1973)
The Lord of the Rings: The Return of the King (2003)
The Lord of the Rings: The Two Towers (2002)
Madagascar (2005)
Marie Antoinette (2006)
Mars Attacks! (1996)
Matilda (1996)
Mulan (1998)
Nacho Libre (2006)
New York Minute (2004)
Ocean's Twelve (2004)
The Order (2003)
Osmosis Jones (2001)
Pirates of the Caribbean: The Curse of the Black Pearl (2003)
Pitch Black (2000)
Pulp Fiction (1994)
Rocky IV (1985)
Sky High (2005)
Skyfall (2012)
Spaceballs (1987)
The Spy Who Loved Me (1977)
Star Wars: Episode I - The Phantom Menace (1999)
The Time Machine (2002)
Titanic (1997)
True Lies (1994)
Unleashed (2005)
Vantage Point (2008)

Other mistakes
 2001: A Space Odyssey (1968)
 Adventures in Babysitting (1987)
 Behind Enemy Lines (2001)
 Blade II (2002)
 Blade Runner (1982)
 Boomerang (1992)
 Bride of Chucky (1998)
 The Call (2013)
 D2: The Mighty Ducks (1994)
 Dangerous Minds (1995)
 Darkman (1990)
 Die Another Day (2002)
 Die Hard (1988)
 Friday the 13th Part 2 (1981)
 From Russia With Love (1963)
 Frozen (2013)
 Gangs of New York (2002)
 Garfield: The Movie (2004)
 The Goonies (1985)
 Halloween 4 (1988)
 Halloween II (1981)
 Harley Davidson and the Marlboro Man (1991)
 Hellfighters (1968)
 The Hunger Games: Catching Fire (2013)
 Into the Storm (2014)
 Into the Wild (2007)
 It's a Wonderful Life (1946)
 Juice (1992)
 The Last Airbender (2010)
 The Little Rascals (1994)
 The Martian (2015)
 The Natural (1984)
 The One (2001)
 The Package (1989)
 Panic Room (2002)
 Paul Blart: Mall Cop (2009)
 Practical Magic (1998)
 A Quiet Place (2018)
 Resident Evil: Afterlife (2010)
 Rocky III (1982)

Snow White and the Seven Dwarfs (1937)
Star Trek IV: The Voyage Home (1986)
Star Wars (1977)
Star Wars: Episode V - The Empire Strikes Back (1980)
Star Wars: The Clone Wars (2008)
Swimfan (2002)
The Tailor of Panama (2001)
Thor (2011)
Tooth Fairy (2010)
Toy Story 2 (1999)
Transformers: Dark of the Moon (2011)
Twister (1996)
The End
More books

CONTINUITY MISTAKES

Something changing from one shot to the next, such as costumes or things in the background.

47 Ronin (2013)

In the scene where the witch gives Mika the dagger to kill herself with, the witch stabs it into the floor. When the witch leaves the dagger is lying on the floor. When Mika goes to grab the dagger it is stuck in the floor again. (01:15:20)

The Addams Family (1991)

The chutes that Wednesday and Pugsley use changes positions when Fester chases Wednesday.

Almost Famous (2000)

Toward the end, Russell goes to talk to William at his house. He turns the chair around to sit on it backwards, and throws the shirt down onto the ground. When he sits down the shirt is back on the chair.

American Pie 2 (2001)

In the scene where John is peeing off Stifler's balcony, he knocks over a plant and knocks out Christy. In the next shot the plant is back, and in the one after that it is gone again. (00:17:15)

American Pie 2
Knocked over plant reappears then vanishes

Universal Pictures

Assault on Precinct 13 (2005)

When Portnow meets with Bishop at the church, in the first closeup of Bishop's crossword puzzle the word "MUD" is the second word across at the top, and at the center of the puzzle the 4-letter word "GEAR" is written in the 5-letter answer - with the fist space left empty. However, in the next closeup of the puzzle, now the word "ETA" is the second word at the top and "MUD" is the third, and the word "GEARS" has the "S" added, with the letter "G" started properly in the first space of the answer. (00:10:15)

Assault on Precinct 13
Crossword changes

Great Movie Mistakes 3

Atlantis: The Lost Empire (2001)

In the beginning scenes, where Milo Thatch is practising his proposal, he slides over (face forward, chest against the board) a chalk drawing of a map detailing the location of Atlantis. When he realises he wiped off the drawing, and sees it on his clothes, he stands in front of the blank part of the chalkboard, "filling in" the space with the map that rubbed off on his shirt - the only problem is, that the image should have rubbed off backwards as he was facing the board when it transferred to his clothes. He could not simply stand in the place of the missing map face forward and have it read properly.

Avengers: Endgame (2019)

In the final battle, Wasp and Ant-Man are in the van trying to get the quantum tunnel operational. We cut back to the fight and we can see Ant-Man there too, fighting in his giant form.

Can't Hardly Wait (1998)

The envelope with the letter for Amanda is suddenly in a very good condition as it ends up in the peanut bowl... even though it has been in the trash, had chewing gum attached to it, been trodden on, had a beer barrel rolled over it, etc....

Charlie's Angels (2000)

When Lucy Liu is climbing a rope up the walls of the bad guy's castle lair, you can clearly see that she is wearing shoes without heels. But later on when she's fighting various bad guys, she's wearing four-inch heels. (01:13:50)

Draft Day (2014)

The owner of the Cleveland Browns drives from NYC to the Teterboro Airport (12 miles from Midtown Manhattan), flies to

Cleveland (450 air miles) and drives to the Browns facility (16 miles) in the time it takes the 2nd, 3rd, 4th and 5th picks in the 1st round of the NFL draft to be made.

Dumb and Dumber (1994)

At the beginning of the movie, Harry's van has bucket seats, yet later on when the "gas-man" rides along, he is sitting on a bench seat in-between Harry and Lloyd. (00:38:00)

Dunkirk (2017)

When the Stukas are shown bombing the beach, they drop a single bomb, but from beach level, you see sticks of bombs landing.

E.T. the Extra-Terrestrial (1982)

When the boys are riding their bikes trying to escape with ET, all the bikes have single brake levers on the right side of their handlebars, but after Elliott shouts that they should follow him to the forest, there's a shot from the POV of one of the bike riders (we know it's not Greg or Elliott) and he has two brake levers on his handlebar.

In the exterior front shots of Elliott's house there are some significant changes to the landscape in different shots. For instance, the two lampposts at the bottom of the driveway change to an entirely different style in some shots, and the huge garden boulders repeatedly vanish and reappear. Also, note when Michael takes off on Elliott's bike to go search for ET, the in-ground lamppost that should be beside the mailbox has vanished, but it reappears when all the government agents are setting things up outside the house.

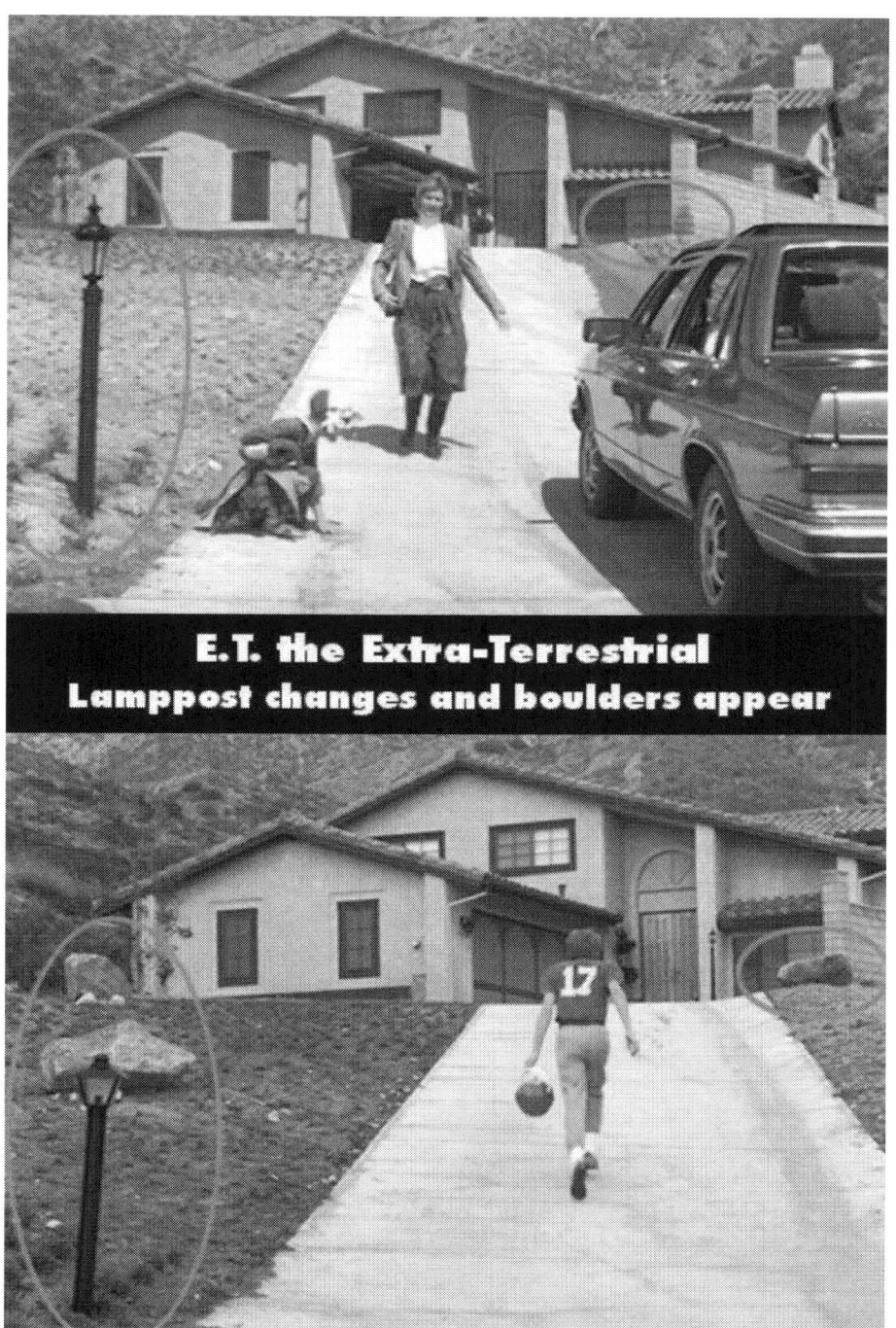

Universal Pictures

Encino Man (1992)

In the convenience store, Link weezes the juice and gets slurpee all over his shirt. He gets kicked out and leaves, but 2 seconds later he comes back in the door and says, "I'll be back". At that point he has nothing on his shirt at all and it's completely dry.

The Evil Dead (1981)

When Cheryl is running through the woods, she is wearing slippers that stay on up until she reaches the cabin door. However, in following shots, she is shown barefoot, and when Ash opens the door her foot is dirty as if she'd been running barefoot the whole time. (00:28:05 - 00:29:10)

The Faculty (1998)

Mr. Furlong pushes Zeke into the fishing tank and it breaks, soaking him from head to toe with water. Moments later they are walking out and he is dry.

The Gift (2000)

In one of the last scenes, Cate Blanchett is standing in the doorway of her son's room. She is wearing a blue striped dress. When she walks into the room, she's wearing a floral dress.

Godzilla (2014)

When Juliette Binoche is running for her life in the tunnel near the beginning of the movie, when the running starts you can see all men run pass Juliette and then she's the last runner. There's even a shot when she's looking back at the leaking water and is last, with no-one behind her. A second later she's in the front of the running group.

Goldfinger (1964)

The T-Bird following Oddjob to the junkyard does not have

fender skirts but does when they give up the chase and head back to the farm. (01:16:25 - 01:20:30)

The Goonies (1985)

On the beach, when Mr. Walsh is tearing up the contract we see the bits of torn paper, but when he tosses them in the air there are many more pieces of torn paper up there.

The Goonies
A few torn bits of paper turn to many

Amblin Entertainment

Happy Gilmore (1996)

When Happy is trying out for the hockey team, he sends a slapshot in front of the coaches and it breaks the glass. In the next shot the glass is intact. (00:04:07)

Happy Gilmore
Glass mends itself (check the reflection)

MCA Universal Home Video

Home Alone (1990)

When Kevin goes to the grocery, he buys Tide detergent. While walking home, the two bags break, but no Tide detergent falls out.

Independence Day (1996)

When General Grey tells the President not to engage until they have visual, in the President's close-up the exterior of this F/A-18 Hornet is quite different than what was shown in the earlier shot, as the canopy closed over him. All the rivets around the canopy have disappeared and the 'danger' triangle is much closer to the name Patrick, the seat differs, etc. Plus the fact that the canopy and hull are actually one unit in the second shot. (02:02:15 - 02:03:15)

Independence Day
F/A-18 canopy rivets vanish, writing differs

Indiana Jones and the Temple of Doom (1984)

When Indy tries to grab the antidote vial from the table, in the closeup just as the vial falls off the table the camera follows the vial as it lands in the empty area to the left of Lao Che's chair where Kao Kan's chair should be, but it's not, and the rug's edge with wood floor beside Lao Che's chair though it shouldn't be. Then Indy hits Kao Kan who is again seated closely to Lao Che's left, as he should be, and when Kao Kan falls backward we see the rug edge is nowhere near Lao Che's chair, also as it should be. (00:08:20)

It (2017)

When Eddie falls through the floorboards, you can see his arm looks perfectly fine and is unbroken in a few quick shots. After the movie cuts back to him a few moments later, suddenly his arm is badly broken. (01:20:30 - 01:23:25)

Jurassic Park (1993)

After the T. Rex rolls Explorer 4 upside-down with Lex and Tim inside, in the closeup when the dinosaur bites on the rubber tire we see the hub hole at the center of the wheel rim, but two shots later the wheel cover is back on the wheel.

Jurassic Park
Yellow wheel cover back on

Universal City Studios

The Little Mermaid (1989)

When Carlotta brings the plates for the meal they all have a dome cover with a top handle, but when Sebastian runs across the table those handles have changed. (00:54:50)

Walt Disney Pictures

Little Nicky (2000)

When the devil is falling apart and his 2nd ear falls off, he tells Nicky he cannot hear him, and asks the demon by his side who catches it to put it back on his head. But towards the end, when the devil is reduced to no more than a mouth and 2 arms, he is able to have a conversation with his demons about what's going on and hear them perfectly. (00:52:05 - 00:58:50)

The Lord of the Rings: The Fellowship of the Ring (2001)

In all five shots, the wax seal on the envelope with the ring is shaped differently. 1st- when Gandalf first seals the envelope with the melted wax. 2nd- when he hands the envelope to Frodo. 3rd- after Gandalf leaves, Frodo looks at the envelope. 4th- when Gandalf returns, Frodo finds the envelope in the trunk and hands it to him. 5th- when Gandalf tosses the envelope into the fire. (00:31:20 - 00:36:40)

New Line Cinema

When the Fellowship meets in Rivendell, and Gimli tries to break the Ring with his axe, the axe breaks into many pieces on the platform upon which the Ring is laid. At first, the pieces are there in the close-up view. When the camera pans back for a long range view of the Fellowship, the pieces of the axe on the platform are gone. In the following close-up, the pieces magically reappear. (01:37:15)

The Matrix Reloaded (2003)

In the car chase scene, when Trinity is driving the cadillac, the Agent in the cop car slams into the driver's side of Trinity's car and the driver's side mirror is bent inwards. When Trinity drives the cadillac onto the exit ramp, the driver's side mirror is back in its normal position.

Warner Bros. Pictures

During the car chase, the twins shoot out most of the windows in the car that Trinity and Morpheus are driving in. But every time they cut to a shot of them inside of the car, the windows are intact and there is no shattered glass to be seen.

Trinity's cut on her right arm disappears and reappears throughout the freeway scene.

During the car chase, one of the Twins shoots at a car behind them to get it out of the way - the right side of the windscreen (as we look at it) is peppered with holes. From another angle, they disappear, only to reappear as it swerves away. (01:25:55)

The Matrix Reloaded
Bullet holes disappear

Warner Bros. Pictures

In the highway chase scene there is a shot of the police cars before they get onto the highway and the cars are Chevrolet Caprices. When they are on the highway chasing Trinity's car, the police cars become brand new Chevrolet Impalas. But when the police cars start to ram her, they become Caprices again.

The Matrix (1999)

When Morpheus is fighting the agent in the bathroom of the building they were trapped in, the agent punches through a brick wall, yet next time we see the wall, there is no damage. (01:24:12)

Warner Bros. Pictures

When they are down on the ground shots they show everyone driving on the right side of the road, but when there are aerial shots, you can see everyone driving on the left side of the road.

In the kitchen scene with Neo and the Oracle, the Oracle is baking cookies. When the Oracle takes the cookies out of the oven and brings them to the table there are 4 cookies on the plate. As she offers a cookie to Neo there are 6 cookies on the plate. (01:14:00)

Warner Bros. Pictures

Miss Congeniality (2000)

At the end of the film when Miss Rhode Island is crowned Gracie tries to take the crown from her. Miss Rhode Island beats her with her bouquet of roses. All of the blossoms are knocked off of the stems. A few seconds later when Gracie is fighting Miss Texas the blossoms are back on the roses that Cheryl, Miss Rhode Island is holding. (01:35:00)

Miss Congeniality
Rose petals reappear back on their stems

Warner Bros. Pictures

Moana (2016)

When Moana is throwing sticks into the ground, after she starts singing, look back at that spot and all the thrown sticks have disappeared.

The Mummy Returns (2001)

In the beginning when Brendan Fraser is looking around the tunnels he turns around to see his kid and they scream. As they are screaming they are at eye level but when a few seconds later when they are standing the kid is like 2 feet shorter then Brendan Fraser, and if you look around there is nothing for the kid to have stood on. (00:05:55)

Universal Pictures

Planes, Trains & Automobiles (1987)

When Del comes out of the passenger side of the dairy truck, he is seen with a black eye, for no reason. The next scene, it is not there. It is there again when he admits to being homeless.

Pretty Woman (1990)

The morning after Vivian's first night at the hotel, room service brings breakfast. When she's eating a croissant it cuts to a shot of Edward, and when it cuts back to Vivian she's eating a pancake which goes from being half done, to being a whole pancake again. (00:30:55)

Pretty Woman
Food changes from croissant to pancake

Buena Vista

Prince of Persia: The Sands of Time (2010)

After being chased by soldiers after talking to his uncle, Dastan gets into a swordfight with Garsiv. As soon as it starts, Garsiv hits a pillar with his weapon knocking a significantly large chunk and a another smaller chunk out of it. In the immediate shot, the size and locations of the two chunks differ.

Red Dragon (2002)

In the scene near the end where Graham and his son are trapped in the bedroom, the Red Dragon attempts to break down the door. After many forceful attempts, we see parts of the door jamb and moulding break-away and stick out from the wall. However, when Mrs. Graham enters the room after the shoot-out, the door jamb and moulding are in perfect condition.

Shallow Hal (2001)

When Hal's co-workers bring him a cake for his promotion, Rosemary takes a slice out for herself. They change shots a couple times, and the size of the piece missing from the cake changes several times, and the layers of the cake change as well.

20th Century Fox

The Simpsons Movie (2007)

When "Emperor" Moe appears in front of Marge, after she and the kids return, the two cartridge belts swung over Moe's shoulders switch from his left over the right, to his right over the left. (01:04:50)

20th Century Fox

Star Wars (1977)

After Darth Vader kills Ben, there's a shot from the docking bay towards him. Vader's lightsaber is missing its red color. [This has been fixed in the 2004 DVD, but is still valid for VHS prints.] (01:28:20)

Star Wars: The Force Awakens (2015)

After Rey's lightsaber battle with Kylo Ren, when the Falcon appears in the wideshot Rey's head is turned to look at the Falcon behind her, to her left, with Finn to her right, but in Rey's two closeups - before and after that wideshot, she's looking straight ahead at the Falcon, with Finn lying directly in front of her. (01:58:50)

The Sum of All Fears (2002)

In the aircraft scenes after the blast in Baltimore, watch the clocks closely. The times go forward, backward, and everything in between.

To All the Boys I've Loved Before (2018)

When Lara Jean and Peter are creating the contract, the writing for the "Ski Trip" changes between when Peter writes it and when they sign the contract.

Top Gun (1986)

When "Charlie" is first introduced to the class, she struts down the aisle in heels. When she follows Maverick into the building, you can briefly see that she is wearing flats to compensate for Maverick's short stature.

Training Day (2001)

Towards the end, Denzel drives his car into 2 cars trying to get Ethan off the hood. After that scene ends you see Denzel driving the same car and the front and rear of the car look nothing like they did when he was crashing into the cars.

Transformers: Revenge of the Fallen (2009)

In Sam's dorm room, there is a white mini fridge at the foot of his bed, flat against the wall under the Cloverfield poster. However, when Sam rushes after Mikaela just as Alice's 'tongue' grabs hold of his neck, that fridge has moved to in front of the closet door, but it moves back to its original position thereafter. (00:50:35 - 00:51:30)

Transformers: Revenge of the Fallen
Fridge moves itself

Paramount/Dreamworks

The Transporter (2002)

When surrounded by police and a garbage truck, Frank drives his car from the overpass onto the passing transport trailer below, then lands behind a hatchback and in front of two cars - a white compact with a sunroof and a grey hatchback. In one specific shot from atop the trailer, as Frank rolls his window down (before he requests the gun) the only vehicle behind Frank's car is the white compact, which is at the trailer's rear. Note things such as the trailer's safety bars, and the view through the compact's windshield for starters. That grey hatchback is back when the ramp is lowered, for the ensuing crashes. (00:08:20)

Twister (1996)

When the cow blows by the truck, the truck is driving down an empty dirt road with water on both sides. During the shots of the occupants, the road behind the truck is paved and dry. Also in one of these rear shots a truck (Red Chevrolet Blazer) drives by in the opposite direction. (00:42:25)

The Untouchables (1987)

When Eliot Ness is at Jim Malone's house for the first time, Malone's collar is opened, then buttoned, then open again.

The Wolverine (2013)

When Viper confronts Shingen, she removes her left glove twice.

X-Men 3 (2006)

When Magneto lands the Golden Gate Bridge on the island, as it hits land it is still very light. When the Brotherhood start to walk toward the island, it cuts to a wide shot of them still walking on the bridge, and it's suddenly dark.

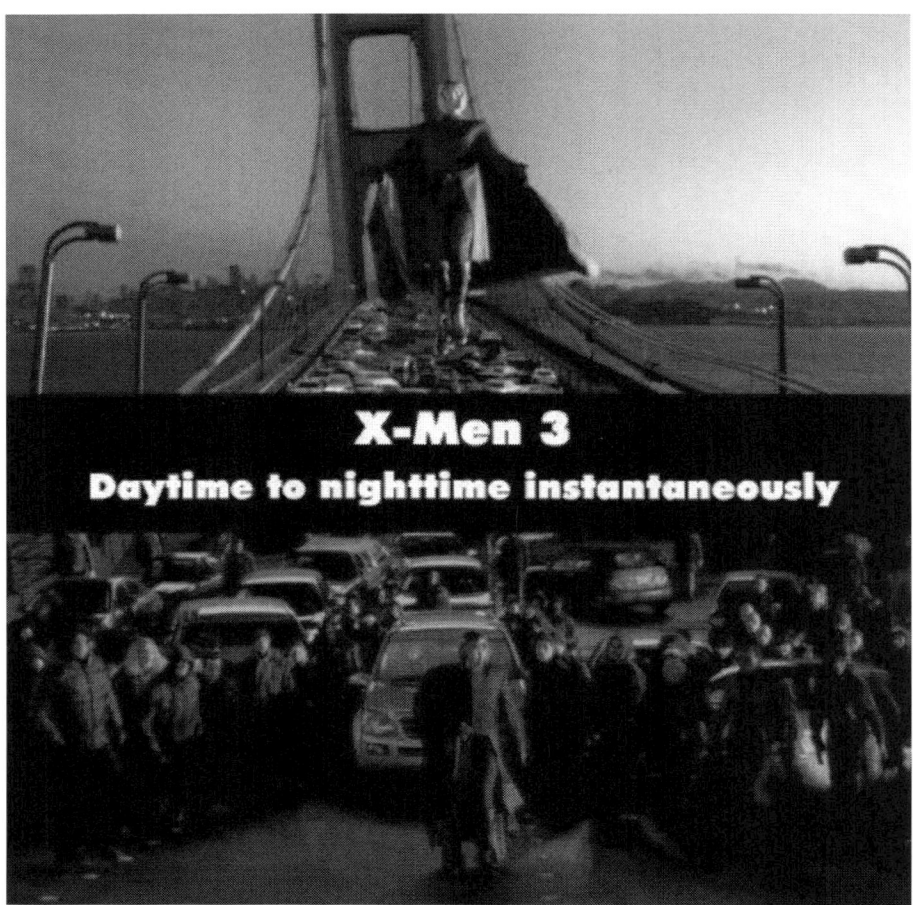

20th Century Fox

VISIBLE CREW/ EQUIPMENT

Crew members, cameras, and other things that don't belong on screen.

Abbott and Costello meet Frankenstein (1948)

During the scene when Lou Costello is reading the narrative on Count Dracula we see the coffin door open and the candle on top of the box starts to descend. By the angle of the coffin door the candle would have easily fallen to the ground. If you look carefully you can see a thin black cord attached to the candle.

American Psycho (2000)

In the scene after Patrick Bateman's second encounter with the detective in his office, we see Bateman having sex at Courtney's apartment. After he rolls off her, Bateman approaches the large, stand-up mirror in the bedroom. In the upper right hand corner of the mirror, a boom microphone can clearly be seen moving around to pick up Christian Bale's lines. The next time we get the same long shot, the microphone is gone. (00:52:45)

Armour of God (1986)

During the final fight scene where Jackie takes on the Amazonian women, there are several shots where dressed up stuntmen double for the women.

Back to the Future (1985)

When Doc Brown loses his footing on the clock tower as it begins to toll, in the next shot, when he swings about towards the clock the thin black stunt cable attached to his waist, that leads around the neck of the statue, is visible. Do not confuse it with the thick silver electric cable Doc is holding. (01:35:25)

Braveheart (1995)

At the funeral of William Wallace's wife, Murron, a white van can be seen. He bends down to kiss her and as he stands back up, if you look over his left shoulder through the trees you can see the van going past. It's very quick, small, and blurred, but it's there. (00:54:25)

Casino Royale (2006)

Bond follows the girl through the streets of Venice. The camera follows him with a track-shot. Bond turns left, going into some kind of alley, and the dolly keeps going. The dolly, camera and crew are reflected in a window for a second. (02:02:10)

Casino Royale
Crew and onlookers reflected in window

Sony

Charlie's Angels (2000)

Right after the race car goes over the bridge the scene changes to the Angels' HQ & there is a close-up of the TV screen that they are watching. As the camera zooms out you can very clearly see the reflection in the TV of the cameraman backing away from the screen with his eye to camera. (00:33:00)

Cheaper by the Dozen (2003)

When Tom and Dylan are hanging from the chandelier, there is a shot of the ceiling showing the chandelier coming loose. Then when it cuts back to Tom hanging from the chandelier, in the background behind him is a crewmember holding a boom mic. (00:24:15)

Cheaper by the Dozen
Boom operator in shot

20th Century Fox

The Descent (2005)

When the girls light the first flare in the cave, the top of a crew-member's head is visible, as he is crouched behind a rock. This is confirmed by Director Neil Marshall on the DVD cast commentary.

In the shot of Holly falling and breaking her leg, a wire can be seen at the top of the frame suspending her down. (00:48:35)

E.T. the Extra-Terrestrial (1982)

When one of the government cars drives alongside the boys on their bikes as they're nearing the bottom of the hill, in the closeup of the car the reflection of a crew member wearing a cap can be seen on the back passenger window, just as the driver speaks into his radio mic and says, "We got 'em," at the start of the shot.

E.T. the Extra-Terrestrial
Crewmember reflected

Universal Pictures

When the two government agents pull over at the bottom of the hill one of the agents remains in the vehicle, and in the shot from inside the car just as Greg rides his bike over it, the crew member's (presumably cameraman) hand can be seen behind the agent's head in the rearview mirror's reflection. (It can't be the driver's hand since it gets blocked from view by the driver's head, within the reflection).

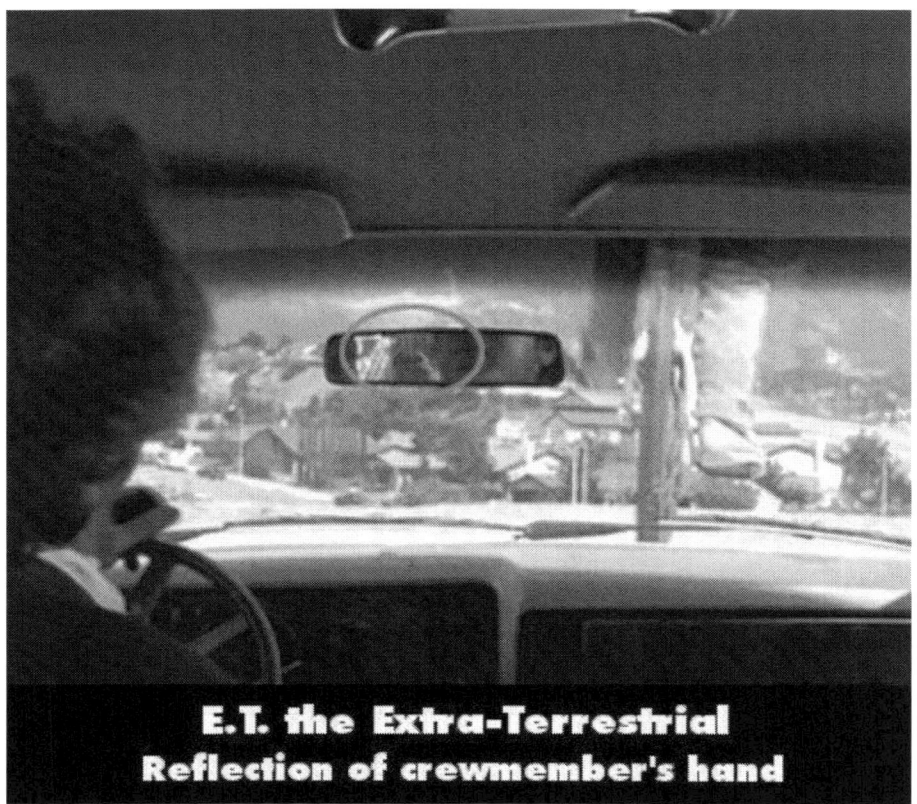

Universal Pictures

Near the start, while the agents are chasing ET, after the last closeup of the jangling keys it cuts to a shot of ET moving fast through the forest and the equipment used to help him move can be seen. This is only visible in the original 1982 unaltered version (such as on Netflix), because ET has been digitally altered in the 2002 version. Interesting to point out that the 2002 2-disc DVD set, which includes the 1982 version, has also been digitally altered in this shot.

The Equalizer 2 (2018)

After burning the car, when Dave takes the trash out there is a camera operator at the end of his driveway. (01:11:00)

Eyes Wide Shut (1999)

In a scene not too long after Tom Cruise attempts to revive a hooker who has OD'd, he is speaking with an older gentleman. The three are in a bathroom and the hooker is passed out on a chair. One of the shower or light fixtures toward the left of the screen is shiny, and in a shot during which the camera briefly tracks in reverse, you can see the camera, cameraman and the focus puller reflected. It's pretty clear and not all that fast.

Face/Off (1997)

In the shoot 'em up scene at the hangar near the beginning of the film, right after Tito and Wanda take down Pollux, when Troy shoots an agent in the stomach and the agent flies back - you can see at least two cable wires pulling him backwards. (00:14:15)

Face/Off
Stunt cables visible

Ferris Bueller's Day Off (1986)

Near the beginning of the movie there is a brief scene around the empty house. While the camera is in the kitchen you can see a reflection of one of the set guys moving in the fridge handle.

A Fish Called Wanda (1988)

When George enters Ken's apartment the first time and Wanda approaches him, if you look in the mirror you should be able to see a crouching crew member wearing a blue shirt. (00:03:15)

Friday the 13th Part 3: 3D (1982)

As Rick and Chris get in the Volkswagon Bug after Shelly returns it, you can see three crew members in the backseat window's reflection. (00:35:55)

When the camera pans past the door, as Chris walks to the cabin, the camera is reflected in the glass windows of the door. (00:22:25)

Harry Potter and the Philosopher's Stone (2001)

Harry, Ron and Hermione run to Hagrid's hut to tell him that they know about the Stone and they knock on the door. As Hagrid opens the door in the first shot looking out, Harry stands behind his tape mark and Hermione and Ron visibly stand behind their shared black tape MARK on the step. (01:38:35)

Warner Bros. Pictures

When the Queen attacks Ron's horse during the chess game, in the shot from behind Ron as he falls, the black straps attached to the horse's left rear leg, used to aid the stunt, are completely visible. (02:05:15)

At the end of term feast, Dumbledore stands and says, "Another year gone." In the next shot of the Gryffindor table, part of the camera equipment is actually visible at the lower right corner of the screen. (01:17:55)

Harry Potter and the Philosopher's Stone
Bit of camera equipment visible

Warner Bros. Pictures

After escaping Devil's Snare, Harry, Ron and Hermione enter the Key room. When Ron says, "You're the youngest seeker in a century." In the next shot of Harry as he grips the broomstick, the wire that it hangs from is clearly visible at its bristles. (01:59:15)

Hellraiser (1987)

When Ashley is running down the corridors before escaping back into her medical room, you can see the dolly that The Engineer chasing her is being pushed on. (01:04:50)

Highlander (1986)

There is no invisible magic power lifting Christopher Lambert in air at the end - there are two wires clearly fixed on his shoulders.

When the Kurgan is fighting Ramerez he hits the wall and stones fall on him. A crew member can be seen pushing the stones out. (00:56:35)

The Hills Have Eyes 2 (2007)

At the start of the film, just after the war exercise, when the Sergeant begins yelling at the recruits you can see the outline of his microphone under his T-Shirt. (It's not his dog tags because you can see the shape and dog tags are not shaped like that.)

The Hurt Locker (2008)

During the scene when Sgt. James is removing the IED from the body cavity of the young boy there is a person standing in the background behind the plastic sheeting.

Independence Day (1996)

When Dr. Okun leads President Whitmore, General Grey, David and the rest to see, as he put it, "The big tamale," the red actor's mark is visible at the top of the landing as they all walk up the ramp. (Only visible on fullscreen DVD.)

Independence Day
Actor's mark visible

20th Century Fox

Indiana Jones and the Temple of Doom (1984)

During Lao Che's car chase, when Short Round pulls up behind the rickshaw and slams on the accelerator, in the next shot just as the car speeds up, we can see the metal bar at the bottom front of the car leading to underneath the rickshaw, for the stunt. Then when the rickshaw crashes we can see the small third wheel at the base of the rickshaw's seat, allowing it to lean all the way back and roll on the ground for the stunt.

Indiana Jones and the Temple of Doom
Stunt's metal bar

Paramount Pictures

Iron Man (2008)

In the extra footage after the credits, the reflection of the crew is visible in the picture frames around the apartment.

Iron Man
Crew reflections

Paramount Pictures

Irreversible (2002)

When Monica is in bed with her boyfriend and they get up to dance, the whole film crew is mirrored on the glass of the window.

Jason Bourne (2016)

When Dewey is introduced and has a phone call with Jeffers about the leak, he is packing away files in a briefcase. On his desk there is a pad of paper beneath Dewey's mobile, and the scripted lines for Dewey's side of the phone conversation are handwritten on the top sheet, not being removed from set prior to filming. (00:08:25)

Jaws (1975)

When the fishermen start out on the hunt, Ben Gardner appears in a close-up leaning on the windshield at forward deck, while talking about how stupid some of the others are. In the next wide shot of the boats, Ben's green boat is towards the left of the screen, and the large reflector screen and camera, that are mounted to the bow of his boat, are visible in front of the forward window where Ben is seen in the previous shot. (00:30:25)

Universal Pictures

Jurassic Park III (2001)

When the group was flying into the island, there's a shot of the plane flying in front of the cloud, and there's the obvious shadow of the helicopter that filmed that shot.

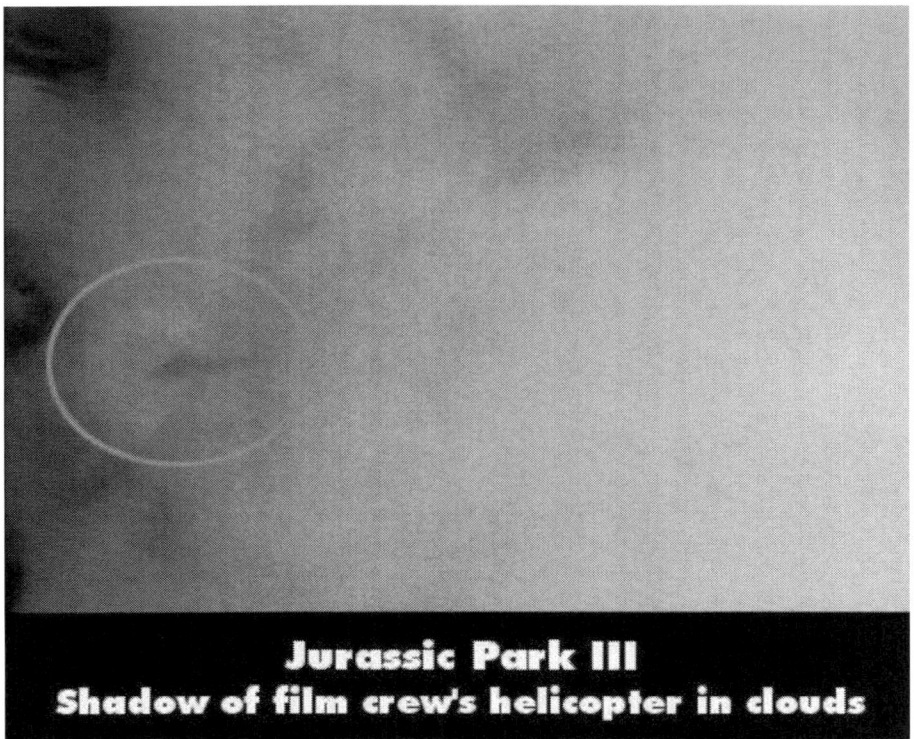

Jurassic Park III
Shadow of film crew's helicopter in clouds

Universal Pictures

King Kong (2005)

On Skull Island, when Carl says, "No one has lived here for hundreds of years," the distinctive reflection of the reflector screen is visible in the lens of Preston's glasses, as he looks down; there are other moments in the film where this happens with characters' eyeglasses.

Labyrinth (1986)

As Sarah, Ludo, Hoggle and Sir Didymus finally walk into Goblin City and reach the fountain, they face the stairs with the surrounding spike walls. In the next two shots, the Goblins appear behind the spiked walls, and in the second shot, on the right, a puppeteer's arm - wearing a short sleeved blue shirt, is amusingly visible under his Goblin soldier puppet; the top of the head of another puppeteer is visible to his right. (01:19:55)

Labyrinth

Puppeteer's blue short sleeve and arm visible

Sony Pictures Home Entertainment

The Lord of the Rings: The Fellowship of the Ring (2001)

After Gandalf removes the One Ring from the fire and places it in Frodo's hand. The large overhead set light is reflected in the Ring, above Frodo's reflection, as he turns it between his fingers in the second close-up of the Ring. (00:37:20)

The Lord of the Rings: The Return of the King (2003)

As Sam carries Frodo on his shoulders, Gollum jumps onto them. When Gollum and Frodo fall down the stairs and then Frodo lies on his back, the black body protector that Frodo wears is first visible at the neck and then under Frodo's front shirt flap that is untucked. (02:37:35)

Mad Max 2 (1981)

When Wez rips the door off the tanker you can see a crouched crew member next to Max. This has been disputed but it is there, watch underneath the steering wheel just after Wez starts shouting "Go! Go! Go!". (01:19:05)

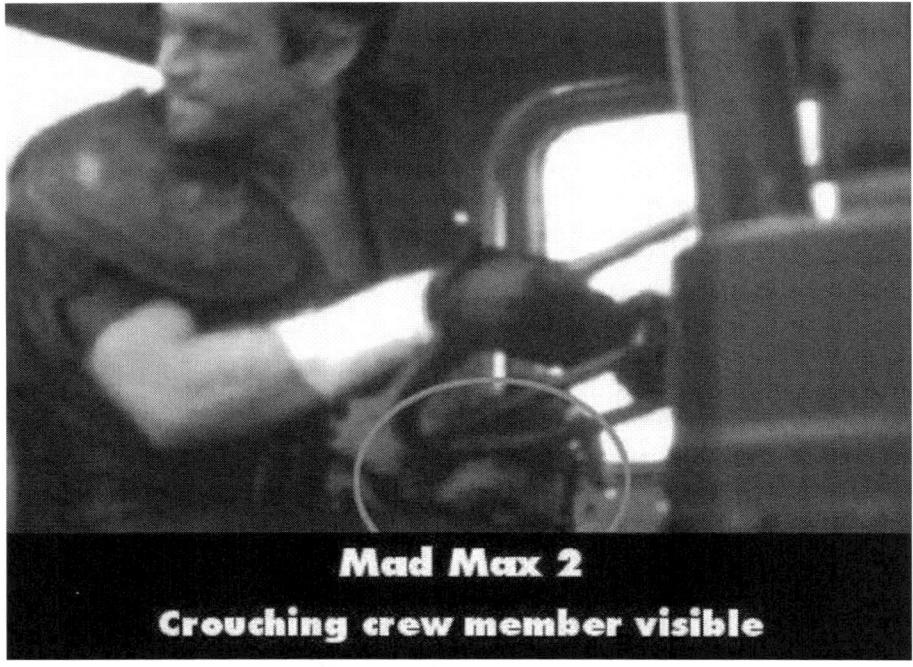

Warner Bros. Pictures

Meet the Fockers (2004)

While passing the frat-house bus, in the close-up, as the two girls are about to flash, the reflections of the camera and two crew members moving on the crew's vehicle are visible on the glass window. (00:14:15)

Minority Report (2002)

When Lamar shoots Witwer it shows the the bullet's point of entry. Looking closely at his shirt, you can see the outline of the square/rectangular blood pack. (01:48:50)

The Outsiders (1983)

When Pony Boy, Dally and Johnny are pulling up to the burning church, just before the first one jumps out of the car if you look through the windshield you can see the water truck that's going to put out the fire after they shoot the scene.

Papillon (1973)

In the last scene where the main character escapes, he jumps into the bay and is supported by a sack which he is carrying. Actually you can clearly see that he is supported from underneath by a diver.

Pearl Harbor (2001)

When Dorie Miller is in the hall of the ship, he is holding a tea or coffee set, on the left side of the screen you can see the hands of the camera focus puller and the wireless focus controller for a brief moment.

The Ring (2002)

In the scene where Noah breaks into the mental institution's record room and is looking through Anna's files, there is a visible arm with a blue sleeve to his right, even though he is alone. (01:06:20)

The Rocky Horror Picture Show (1975)

When the newlyweds leave, just as Ralph and Betty drive their car towards the camera, the reflection of the boom mic/pole is visible on the car's windshield. (00:06:40)

The Rocky Horror Picture Show
Visible reflection of boom mic/pole

20th Century Fox

Rocky III (1982)

Just before the second fight with Clubber and just after the pre-fight brawl, when the camera switches to the shot of Rocky and Apollo you can see a director's chair at the top left of the screen with "Mr. T" written on it. (01:22:50)

Rush Hour 2 (2001)

When Carter is fighting Zhang Ziyi, she thrusts a sword into his coat. For a split second, there is a shot where a man is crouched down behind the statue on which Carter is against, looking up at Carter and Zhang Ziyi. (01:13:45)

Saw 3D (2010)

When Hoffman runs to hide from the second coroner, he goes right up close to the camera. When he does, you can see the camera's shadow on his face. (01:08:00)

Saw V (2008)

In the crushing room at the end of the film, Strahm is trying to open the box where Hoffman is. As it's descending into the ground, on the side of the box you can see the feet of a crew member with white sneakers moving around. It is not Strahm's feet: he's wearing black boots. No slow-mo is required.

Speed (1994)

When the bus is about to jump the bridge, you can see that the bridge is flat, apart from the broken part, but when the bus jumps over the bridge, there's wood and stuff piled up at the end, making it "kick". (01:03:35)

Spider-Man 2 (2004)

In the very last scene of Mary Jane looking over the city in Peter's apartment, there is a reflection in the window where the camera lens and cameraman are partially visible.

Split (2016)

In the second scene where the main character approaches the car, there's the filming crew visible in the right corner of the car's bumper. (00:02:30)

Star Wars (1977)

When the Falcon is in the Death Star hangar, a scanning crew is sent aboard to find passengers, one of the stormtroopers walks straight past the camera and its shadow is visible on his leg. (01:01:55)

Stargate (1994)

Throughout the movie, in the shots of the guys on the alien planet, the white reflector screens and film crew's reflections are visible in their sunglasses. (00:40:20)

Stargate
Camera crew visible in sunglasses

Artisan Home Entertainment

Top Gun (1986)

When Goose and Maverick are in the sea after their plane crashes, look carefully, there's a thin black rope latching onto Maverick and the camera crew's boat.

When Charlie walks down to the front of the class in the hanger, Jester is the only one at the front. Look at the reflection of Maverick's glasses, and the reflection shows lots of people standing in front of him.

Troy (2004)

After the Trojans let loose their arrows on the Myrmidons who have just reached their shores, there is a close-up of a Myrmidon stuntguy as he slams onto the sand, beside the ship. At the start of this shot a crew member (who is stooping) is visible on deck, at the bow of the ship. (Use slo-mo if necessary.) (00:39:50)

FACTUAL ERRORS

Historical/geographical mistakes, or other real world errors.

2010 (1984)

While the Leonov has a centrifugal section to simulate gravity, the ship's bridge is not part of it (evidenced by the stationary views outside its portholes). Yet in various scenes, including the one when Floyd rushes in to discuss his plan to return to Earth sooner with Tanya, gravity seems quite evident. Floyd marches across the compartment onto the raised pilot area's floor, then steps down from it, his foot landing audibly. Tanya's open jacket also hangs down normally as she moves about. Yet when Floyd demonstrates his plan using two pens, they float in mid air. (01:26:50)

Along Came a Spider (2001)

As the kidnapper is watching TV, we hear a news anchor describing the kidnapped child. She is described as 12 years old, 3 ft. 5 in. tall, and 52 pounds. This is the size of a child half this age. A 12 year old of this size would be freakishly small, which this character is not. And as we see her throughout the movie, she is easily approaching 5 feet tall and in the 70 - 80 pound range.

Armageddon (1998)

When A.J. starts up the Armadillo to jump the canyon, you can hear the sound of big, internal combustion engines. The Armadillo must have electric engines in order to function in the vacuum of space. Electric engines are virtually silent. (01:47:55)

Body Heat (1981)

Under US law neither Peter Lowenstein nor Oscar Grace would be allowed any level of participation in the investigation, arrest and prosecution of Ned Racine. Both have a highly visible social relationship with him, which disqualifies them from having anything to do with a criminal case against him. In fact as soon as he became a suspect in Edmund Walker's murder they would both be officially 'warned off' - told not to contact him again for any reason.

Bohemian Rhapsody (2018)

In a scene in 1980, Brian May is teaching everyone the beat for his new song "We Will Rock You." However that song was released in 1977.

Broken Arrow (1996)

The United States Air Force does NOT, ever, allow its pilots to box competitively! Ground staff, yes; pilots, no, never. A pilot can be suspended from flying if he/she receives a blow to the head in day-to-day life; boxing is right out. Almost all air forces (the RAF included) impose this rule.

Casino Royale (2006)

In the scenes at Miami airport you see numerous CSA planes (Czech Airlines). Czech Airlines offer no direct flights to Miami, however Prague airport, where this scene was shot, is full of CSA planes. (00:44:50)

Catch Me If You Can (2002)

In the scene where Handratty hits the button to stop the press, suddenly individual checks come flying up from the press. This could not happen. On such a large press the checks would be printed several up on a large sheet of paper, to be cut down after printing is completed. (01:53:10)

The Core (2003)

The geodes occurring in the mantle during the film are impossible in two ways. Firstly, there are no gaps at those depths. The pressure is approximately 3.5 million times surface pressure, and it is not feasible that such structures could form, let alone be maintained. Secondly, the crystals inside the geodes are described as amethysts. Amethysts are a purple variety of quartz, and as any undergrad geology student could tell you, there is no quartz in the mantle, it simply is not stable at such high temperatures.

Dead Poets Society (1989)

The film takes place in a private boarding school the 1950's, however one of the students is studying from a 1980's chemistry textbook.

Die Another Day (2002)

Towards the end of the film as the helicopter tumbles through the sky after it has fallen out of the plane, Jinx looks back from the cockpit and sees the diamonds in a neat pile spilling out of the door. Surely if the helicopter has been tumbling through the sky, they would be scattered all over the place. (01:59:10)

Die Another Day
Helicopter falls but diamonds stay in place

MGM Pictures

Django Unchained (2012)

Dr Schultz pays with 12 $1000 bills, but $1000 bills were not created until 1861, after the time period of this movie.

Dunkirk (2017)

In the silent overfly of the plane that ran out of fuel in the background you see a lot of modern architecture that is definitely not from the 1940s. (01:30:15)

When the boat returns to England they state the cliffs are Dorset. There were 3 evacuation routes from Dunkirk - all to Kent.

It would be nonsense to sail from Dunkirk to Dorset as you have to almost pass Dover on the way. Never mind the fact the boat would probably not have made it without refuelling.

Near the start of the film in the harbour when the camera pans around to the left looking out to sea, you can see the back of the modern Weymouth Lifeboat 17-32 moored up in the background.

Elektra (2005)

When Elektra closes her cell phone on McCabe, a dial tone can be heard. Cell phones don't have dial tones. Even if they did, Elektra hung up, so nothing would be heard.

First Man (2018)

The interior shots of the Gemini and Apollo Spacecraft show worn and dirty panels, knobs, switches and circuit breakers. The movie most likely used some original cockpit trainers, but in reality the astronauts were flying brand new spacecraft that were spotless.

When they are in quarantine after returning to Earth, they are in a room with several magazines. One of the magazines is an issue of National Geographic with the cover image of them standing on the moon. That is the December 1969 issue of National Geographic, whereas they were actually in quarantine in late July/early August 1969.

Furious 7 (2015)

When we see Shaw at the hospital it is in London. However, the plugs above the bed are two pronged American style outlets. (00:01:15)

Girl, Interrupted (1999)

When Suzanna and Lisa are at Daisy's house, Daisy lays out

money for Lisa so that she can get pancakes, and the bill she laid down is one of the new bills. This movie is set in the 60s so of course they wouldn't have the new bills, considering they didn't start making them until 1998.

Gladiator (2000)

In one of the scenes in Rome leading up to a fight, leaflets are being handed out. These didn't exist, event notices were written up on boards. (01:02:15)

Gravity (2013)

When Ryan enters the space station and removes her spacesuit she is shown wearing only a tank top and boy shorts. In reality, according to NASA's official webpage astronauts wear a liquid cooling and ventilation garment and an absorption garment (space diapers) under their suit. (00:38:45)

The shuttle's original mission was to service Hubble, yet when the shuttle is wrecked, Kowalsky moves with Stone to the ISS, which just happens to be "a short hike away." Hubble orbits at an altitude of 350 miles/560km, while the ISS does so at an altitude of about 250 miles/410km. Furthermore, even if they had been able to see the ISS from Hubble's orbit, they would have only seen it speed ahead, as their orbital velocities are very different: 7.66km per second for the ISS and 7.5km per second for Hubble. (00:23:20)

Green Berets (1968)

The final scene of the movie has Col. Kirby and the little Vietnamese boy supposedly on the beach at Da Nang, Vietnam. Kirby is saying, "The future of 'nam is you, kid", and the camera pans out to the sea and the sun is going down. The sun's sinking in the east...

Green Book (2018)

Opening scene shows NYC 1962 as a 1964 Chevy Impala rolls by.

Hallowed Ground (2007)

When the cop saves the girl from the mob of locals, his car tires squeal as he accelerates away, but the car is on loose dirt, which makes the squealing impossible.

Halloween (2007)

Federal institutions have strict rules for inmates or patients based on the reason for their incarceration, including substituting metal utensils with safer plastic ones. Despite being convicted of brutally killing his family, Myers is still trusted with a sharp metal fork - resulting in the nurse's death.

Halloween: The Curse of Michael Myers (1995)

No electricity, yet the washer is running.

High Noon (1952)

During the gun battle, Gary Cooper runs behind a building that has an air-conditioner or swamp cooler installed in a second-floor window. (01:17:30)

Hollow Man (2000)

Rats have very poor eyesight but an extremely keen sense of smell. The rat introduced into the gorilla's cage would know right away that there was another animal in the cage and would never scamper happily into danger, as this one does.

The Hurt Locker (2008)

When SGT Sanborn is placing the items in the white box, you can see his special skill badges. He has an EOD badge placed above his Combat Infantryman's Badge which should never happen. While it is possible for an EOD member to have a CIB (second MOS), no badge is ever worn above the CIB, EIB, or CAB. (00:09:25)

Indiana Jones and the Kingdom of the Crystal Skull (2008)

The movie supposedly is set in 1957, yet Mutt's motorcycle is based on a 2000 or newer Harley Davidson softail, showing the modern-day controls and Twin Cam motor, instead of the pan-head motor that would have been the period-correct engine for 1957. It also has a front disc brake - you can see the master cylinder on the handlebars. Again, out-of-place on a 1957 bike.

Indy and Mutt fly to Nazca, Peru. Nazca is only 4 hours away on bus from the capital Lima, yet the city they show on the movie is Cuzco, which is 24 hours away from Lima. Cuzco is on the east side of the country, Nazca is on the west coast right next to Lima. Also, back in 1957 only Lima had an airport, yet they show a Nazca airport that didn't exist.

It (2017)

Eddie specifically tells the gang not to take his mom's "Delicious Deals" snacks because his mom loves them. But Delicious Deals are made by Mrs. Freshley, a company that was not founded until 1994. The boxes used in the movie even include the modern design that can be found today in most Dollar Tree stores. (00:23:00)

Joe Kidd (1972)

When the posse arrives at the mission, a horizontal jet stream can be seen during this scene. (01:00:00)

Kingsman: The Secret Service (2014)

When the barracks are completely flooded, several of the trainees shove shower hoses down the toilets for an "unlimited supply of air" (as Merlin explains moments later, describing it as "simple physics"). However, that old fireman's trick is a technique for surviving dense smoke, which is not under tons of pressure. In the barracks flooded 9 feet deep with water, the pressure would be so enormous that it would easily gush straight down the toilets in a powerful torrent, eliminating any "unlimited air supply."

Left Behind (2014)

When TCAS sounds on an airliner, it should include instructions for the pilot to climb or descend. The pilot should not have to call another plane to inform that pilot. It would take too much time.

Mission: Impossible (1996)

The vents that Hunt and his sidekick crawl down at CIA Head-quarters are standard galvanized iron box vents; they are very common in the building trade. Try walking or crawling down one - you'll make a noise like the sky is falling down. People will be able to hear you for miles. Every person in that build-ing would know somebody crawling about in the vent system. (This error applies to dozens of films, not only this one).

Murder on the Orient Express (2017)

At beginning at the Wailing Wall in Jerusalem in 1936, we see the large plaza at the Western Wall. In 1936 this was only a nar-row lane. The plaza was enlarged only after June 1967.

The Outsider (2018)

At the point where Jared Leto is released from prison he is picked up in a 1960 Black Chrysler Imperial. As the camera rises it shows the date as 1954. The car is used a few more times in the movie.

Pain & Gain (2013)

The movie is set around 1995. But the SWAT team in the movie is wearing gear from the 2000s. (MICH-2000 helmet, modular tactical vest, M4 variant with picatinny rails and scope). Plus, in a scene when the guys are shopping for a taser (gun shop scene), some of the rifles on display are from 2000s era. AR-15 variants with variant stock, foregrip and picatinny rail. Those style of weapon system were unheard of in early 90s. Even Special Forces just adopted it by the late 90s.

The Peacemaker (1997)

The Russians stopped using steam locomotives in the 1970's. So bringing one out of retirement in 1997 to haul nuclear warheads would mean that your highly secret nuclear train would be well known among rail enthusiasts for weeks before.

Pink Floyd The Wall (1982)

In World War 2 London, Pink is shown playing with an aeroplane model - an Avro York. The earliest available plastic model kit of this aircraft was produced in 1967. Inaccurate model aside, it begs the question of what a kid of Pink's age would be doing with a plastic model kit during World War 2 anyway.

Pokemon 3: The Movie (2000)

In "Pikachu and Pichu," when Pikachu and the Pichu brothers come to the big play structure thing, there are a bunch of Pokemon around, including a red-and-white, ball-shaped Pokemon called Voltorb. The dubbers for the English version made a very noticeable error here: instead of Voltorb saying "Voltorb," (almost all Pokemon say parts of their names when they speak) it says "Electrode," which is the name of a similar-looking, but different Pokemon. The two are both red and white, but the difference is that Voltorb has eyes on the red part of its body, while Electrode has eyes on the white part of its body.

Red Tails (2012)

The German fighters depicted in the film are Messerchmitt Bf 109 G-6s, and every single one of them is using the Rüstsatz VI gun pod, that is, 2 extra 20mm Mg 151 cannons. The Luftwaffe only equipped their Bf 109s with the gun pods when they were going to intercept bombers. In this movie, even on the fighter vs fighter missions, they have these gun pods, which is inaccurate, because the gun pods dramatically reduced the turning performance of the Bf 109s.

Before receiving the North American P-51D Mustangs, the Red Tail squadron was using the Curtiss P-40E Warhawk. The movie shows the Warhawks being able to keep up with the German Bf 109 G-6s quite easily, fighting on even terms. In reality, the Bf 109 G-6 could easily outperform the Warhawk, being able to easily outrun and out-turn the Warhawk. Still, the Bf 109s are no match for the Warhawks.

Ronin (1998)

When Gregor shoots the guy in the car after nearly killing the little girl, blood sprays over the window, but there's no bullet hole. If the bullet exited his head, hence spraying blood, it should have gone through the window too. (00:55:00)

Rush (2013)

Lauda is an Austrian. Yet when his name appears on scoreboards with his country abbreviation, it shows AUS, which is for Australia. AUT is for Austria.

San Andreas (2015)

In the film, the San Andreas fault produces the largest, most sensational earthquake in earth history that levels both Los Angeles and San Francisco, also creating a massive tsunami that also floods the latter. In reality, and according to many earth-quake experts, the biggest quake that this fault could produce is an 8.3 and, being a land and not ocean fault, cannot cause a tsunami. Or as consultant to the film Tom Jordan, director of the Southern California Earthquake Center stated, "I gave (the filmmakers) free advice, some of which they took... But much of which they didn't - magnitude nines are too big for San Andreas, and it can't produce a big tsunami."

The Santa Clause (1994)

Finishing his rounds on the morning of Christmas Day, flying over downtown Chicago, the sun is over the horizon west of Chicago, Sunrises occur in the east, not the west. (00:26:10)

The Social Network (2010)

When Mark types email addresses in to tell people about facemash, he writes to several people @harvard.edu. At the time the movie takes place, undergraduate email addresses were all of the form username@fas.harvard.edu. Furthermore, the network brought down by facemash would have been re-ferred to as the FAS network. (FAS stands for Faculty of Arts and Sciences; the eponymous network covered all buildings within the College and Graduate School of Arts and Sciences.).

Species (1995)

Fitch, who professes qualifications in biology, genetics and biochemistry, says that they made Sil female because she's a natural predator and so she'd be more docile. He should retake his finals. In every single species of predator on earth - every single one - the females are the hunters, aggressors and killers. The males may be socially dominant but they are the 'docile' ones. There are no exceptions - and no human DNA was used to create Sil - they used synthetic DNA based on the instructions trans-mitted to them.

Spider-Man: Homecoming (2017)

When the bus is shown entering Washington, DC for the competition, the shot shows the bus traveling over the Arlington Memorial Bridge with the Lincoln Memorial in the background. That bridge is on the southwest side of the city. Since NYC is to the northeast of DC, this means that to get to that bridge and enter DC that way, the bus had to drive all the way around the city and then come back in from the opposite direction. Even if the bus driver made a mistake and missed the most direct route into the city from the north, there are dozens of other ways to get to the heart of the city without adding a good 45 minutes to an hour to the trip.

Spy Game (2001)

In the scene where Brad Pitt meets Robert Redford on the roof of a house in Berlin in (I think it was) 1980, you can see a lot of GSM transmitters. GSM cell transmitters didn't come until 1993.

Stripes (1981)

Even in the '80s obesity was a strict disqualification for military service. John Candy wouldn't have had a chance of passing the required medical.

The Sum of All Fears (2002)

In the scene where the dock worker receives the e-mail stating 'the day has arrived', the e-mail is dated Mon, 19 Nov 2002. However, November 19 2002 was a Tuesday.

Time Bandits (1981)

When the Titanic sinks all six dwarves and Kevin end up in the sea clutching a lifebelt. The water in which the Titanic sank was freezing - that is how most of the casualties died, by freezing, not drowning. In water like that you'd be lucky to stay conscious for more than a few minutes. Despite this none of them show the slightest effect of the cold. Maybe the dwarves have some 'magical' ability to withstand lethal cold, but Kevin doesn't even react to being plunged into freezing cold water. He'd be screaming in pain, but he doesn't even show the slightest sign of discomfort.

Under Siege (1992)

When the ship launches the missile to take out the satellite building in Hawaii they shoot a Harpoon Missile. The Harpoon is a anti-ship missile, it also is a fire and forget missile that flies in a straight line. In the movie it shows on the radar the missile making a turn, that would never happen.

Who Framed Roger Rabbit (1988)

The picture of Eddie and Teddy on the road with dad, supposedly taken in 1906, shows a Ringling Bros and Barnum & Bailey circus poster. In 1906, the Ringling Brothers circus and the Barnum & Bailey circus were two separate circuses playing in different parts of the country. They did not combine the two shows until 1919. (00:27:00)

Yes Man (2008)

All the Cisco VoIP phones seen in the film have the booting Cisco logo on them and would not work due to no connection.

PLOT HOLES

Events or character decisions which only exist to benefit the plot, rather than making sense.

2012 (2009)

During the later parts of this movie there is much talk about 'continental displacement' and this appears to be happening in the film. The Earth's crust is falling apart because of the heating of the inner core, and all the cities seems to be falling apart since the ground can no longer hold them. When our cast finds themselves surprised to be already over China when they figured to be over the ocean, it is explained that Asia has actually moved from where it was. If this phenomenon is taking place globally, how come the monks in China don't seem to have been disturbed at all? In fact the bell the monk rings as the ocean approaches hasn't even been shaken. The arks are built in between the mountains, but the mountains are apparently fine. Shouldn't they be falling like the rest of the crust?

Blue Thunder (1983)

Apart from the impressive pyrotechnics, what is the point of destroying the Blue Thunder helicopter? By far the most expensive, time consuming and technically complex part of producing any aircraft is the design and development phase - once the prototype is in the air production is relatively straightforward. The bad guys can make new Blue Thunders any time they like, and Murphy has destroyed the only evidence he has that there was a criminal conspiracy behind the whole programme - the 'videotape' he has of blurry, false coloured characters will convince nobody. Without the helicopter to back him up that tape is of no value to him.

Brave (2012)

During the scene where Merida gives her speech on "breaking tradition", her mother, as a bear, moves silently behind the majority of the crowd, so they don't see her. Fair enough. However, Merida and her father's clan are all looking in the same general direction (towards the crowd) while she's speaking - how does no one from Merida's clan see a bear moving at the back of the room?

Bring it On (2000)

In the final cheerleading sequence for the Toros, it is obvious that the middle stunt falls. Instead of reshooting, they kept the mistake in. The team wouldn't have been "up there" with the Clovers if it were an actual competition.

Brother Bear 2 (2006)

The whole plot of the first "Brother Bear" was that Kenai had to go to that mountain to become human. But at the end of this movie, the spirits were about to change Kenai back into a human in the middle of a cliff, which makes the entire first movie completely pointless.

Bumblebee (2018)

How can Bumblebee and Optimus already have the car specs and colours before they leave Cybertron for the first time to come to earth? Optimus didn't have this when they came to earth in the first Transformers movie.

Capricorn One (1977)

For such a well-financed, well-organised bunch of ruthless

killers the people who try to clean up the mess that NASA leaves behind seem to have the intelligence of a cheese sandwich. 'Disappearing' one of their employees - the one who works out the discrepancy in the triangulation of the radio signals - is an obvious necessity but replacing him with a woman who claims to have lived in his apartment for years is stupid beyond explanation. The reporter knows that she is lying - it's as if they wanted to confirm that his suspicions of a conspiracy were true (and hence worth investigating). What is to stop him checking with the man's neighbours, or local shops? What about his bank, credit card suppliers, utility companies, friends and family who would have been in contact with him at that address? What about the landlord, or the mortgage company, or vehicle or driver's licence registration? What about the local electoral roll? There would be official records going back to the day he moved in to the apartment, and neither NASA nor their hired killers could have accessed all of that information even if they knew about it.

When the three astronauts escape and steal the Learjet, they could get on the aircraft's radio and announce themselves, at least on the Mayday frequency if not to a control tower somewhere.

Changing Lanes (2002)

When Ben Affleck is meeting with the man who changes Samuel Jackson's credit record, the man remarks that Samuel Jackson should not have told Ben Affleck that he was in insurance. Samuel Jackson never told Ben Affleck that he was in insurance.

Charley Varrick (1973)

Swapping his dental X-ray records with his deceased partner won't convince anyone that Varrick is dead - then (as now) the patient's name appears on the X-ray.

Child's Play (1988)

Andy is suspected of having killed Eddie Caputo, because he was at the scene when Eddie's house blew up and Eddie was killed. But there are glaring things that go unquestioned: None of the cops seem to think it's strange that a six-year-old kid would travel by himself so far to some random house in order to blow it up. The South Side neighborhood where Eddie lives is halfway across the city from Andy's apartment. How did Andy know where Eddie lived? How do the cops think he even knew Eddie at all? None of them address this most puzzling problem.

Cliffhanger (1993)

This happens after Gabe has killed the guy in the cavern and is reaching for the radio. We hear Frank trying to reach them, so they must be on the same frequency. Then, Hal finds out that a bomb has been planted, grabs a radio from the bad guys and starts yelling for Gabe to get out of the cavern because of the bomb. Why didn't Frank hear any of this on his headset?

Con Air (1997)

At the end of the film when Cyrus is handcuffed to the ladder of the fire truck, he crashes through a restaurant bridge and falls towards the road below, (the fire truck passes below him) but somehow he lands in a construction yard on a conveyer belt leading to a crusher. (01:39:43)

The Core (2003)

In the melting bridge scene, the space microwave was powerful enough to melt the bridge's thick metal but how come it could not melt the roof of the cars on the bridge? (01:27:10)

Days of Thunder (1990)

I have never seen a Daytona 500 race where the winner is immediately left completely alone and is able to walk over to his crew chief who is still at the pit wall and hold a quiet conversation.

Die Hard 2 (1990)

The whole of Col. Stuart's plot to free General Esperanza and flee to a country with no US extradition laws would be rather impossible, as the plane with Esperanza and the terrorists would have been brought down by the US Air Force long before reaching international waters, especially given the fact that they would not maintain control over the airport landing systems after taking off.

The Eagle Has Landed (1976)

Radl and Steiner discuss the entire scheme to kidnap Churchill on the Alderney docks - in full view and hearing of a number of civilians (who shouldn't be there, pace another posting), including local fishermen. Though the Germans banned all fishing activities in the Channel islands including Alderney in 1941, they were well aware that there was a flow of information from the island to military authorities in the mainland. Why would they be so stupid as to discuss a top secret military mission in public? In reality, they wouldn't even discuss it in front of their own men.

The Equalizer 2 (2018)

Robert first shoots the electrical transformer on the pole's top, then enters the bakery, slices the wheat sacks and uses electrical fans to create a dust cloud for a dust explosion. How are the electrical fans supposed to work after the electricity is cut?

A Fish Called Wanda (1988)

Archie goes from being waist-deep in a barrel of oil to walking onto the airplane and sitting next to Wanda. She greets him, etc. But there's no oil on his pants, no logical question by Wanda: What the heck happened?

The Fly (1986)

In any given volume of air, there are any number of tiny, living organisms; dust mites, viruses, bacteria, etc. Why did the tele-porter combine Seth's DNA only with the fly that was in the chamber? If he had taken the "floating organisms" into account in his calculations and programming, then why would he not have excluded ALL foreign DNA?

Friday the 13th Part 3: 3D (1982)

We see Jason get his outfit from Harold's clothes line. Yet in Chris's flashback Jason has these same clothes already on.

The Game (1997)

When Nick confronts the P.I. and yells "Why are you following me?", he looks inside the car and see the file with his picture on the front seat. The P.I. notices this and turns the file over. After Nick grabs his gun, the P.I. jumps out on the other side, raises his hands in the air and tells him someone hired him and runs off. As the P.I. runs off, Nick yells "Who hired you?" as he stands alone next to the car. He then waits a minute and walks off. If he really wanted to know more information, he could have taken the file that was right in front of him on the carseat. It makes no sense that he is desperate for information about the strange events that are going on, sees this file on him, and yet doesn't even pick it up or look at it. (00:59:55)

Gothika (2003)

In the scene where she goes to her house after escaping there is no police tape on the front door even though it is a crime scene. Earlier the police searched and taped her office - it only makes sense that they would do the same to her house.

Halloween 5 (1989)

In the beginning, Rachel and Loomis are referring to Rachel's mother as being Jamie's step mother and Rachel refers Jamie as being her step sister. Rachel's mother is Jamie's foster mother and Jamie is Rachel's foster sister as said in Halloween 4.

Happy Gilmore (1996)

In the final tournament when Happy is stuck in the rough, he swings five times. Assuming he hit his drive into the rough and hit an AMAZING shot from the edge of the water into the hole, he still could do no better than a seven on the hole. Happy only lost one stroke on the hole. (01:16:50)

Home Alone 4 (2002)

In the scene when the robbers first enter the house, Kevin goes to hide in the shower. It looks like there is only one way out of the shower. How can Kevin possibly get out of the shower, let alone the bathroom, without getting wet after he turns it on?

Hostel (2005)

Theres no way Paxton could have took the bodies off the cart, laid them down, and stacked them back on top of him in the 3 seconds it took for the guy to open the door. (01:07:15)

Inside Out (2015)

Joy and Sadness are stuck outside of the control center. They are trying to figure out how to get back, and encounter maintenance workers who are discarding old memories. The maintenance workers show that they have the power to send memories back up to the control center to be played. Why couldn't they send the core memories that Joy had back up the same way? Better yet, why not use that method to send Joy and Sadness back up to the control center? The director of the film is even aware of the plot hole, and said "Yeah, well then we wouldn't have a third act," before explaining how the idea of recalling memories was added in later, "box[ing] [the screenwriters] in a corner a little bit."

The Italian Job (1969)

Why on earth do they drive the Minis up the ramps into the bus while it is moving? They are on a long, straight, relatively quiet stretch of road, but there are cars and buildings about. That ramp is going to make a noise like the sky coming down (we see sparks as it scrapes on the road) and they put on a display anyone would be, frankly, amazed to see. Don't they think one single person would call the police? Don't they think that reports of three brightly coloured Minis will be connected with the recent robbery? They cannot possibly think they have to load the Minis on the run in order to elude the police; they have lost the police cars and are no longer being pursued. Why not just park the bus on the hard shoulder and drive the Minis sedately up that ramp? An unusual sight, maybe, but nowhere near as clumsy, obvious and attention-getting as the way they do it. They are asking to be pulled over and arrested.

Jaws (1975)

When Hooper and Chief Brody are trying to get the Mayor to re-close the beach after finding Ben Gardner's boat, they fail to mention they also found Ben Gardner's severed head. The Mayor would be forced to re-close the beach if yet another confirmed shark fatality had been mentioned, but Hooper and Brody never bring that important detail up. [This is still a mistake, but the explanation for this is that the scene where they find Ben Gardner's head was not in the original script. Originally, they just found his boat. Spielberg felt the scene needed a little more shock value so they shot the part with the head in a swimming pool long after the main filming had been completed.] (00:50:20)

Jumping Jack Flash (1986)

When Terry gets back to her computer, after escaping from the spies and cops, the time is after 3pm New York time. If Jack actually is in Russia or Eastern Europe, wouldn't he have already gone to, and been killed at, that 5pm meeting?

Jurassic World: Fallen Kingdom (2018)

There was only one T-Rex on the island. When Owen and the others are running down the side of the island escaping the volcanic ash, another dino tries to eat them but then the T-Rex shows up and kills it. This establishes the T-Rex was there in that spot. Owen and the others then wash up back on shore and find the soldiers loading the dinos on a boat and stow away. Then when Blue is bleeding out they have to get a blood transfusion and the only viable candidate is the T-Rex who is now captured and sedated on the ship. How did the soldiers capture, let alone bring the Rex to the ship from where it was seen by Owen back up over hills and rocky terrain? It would have been an all day process just to haul the T-Rex to the ship. It just magically appears on the ship after they stow away on it and can provide the blood Blue needs.

The Karate Kid III (1989)

Daniel first needs Miyagi's signature (which Miyagi refuses) to enter the tournament. However the rest of the movie focuses on Daniel's signature needed to enter instead. Didn't Miyagi officially need to sign? How did it suddenly switch?

Kiss the Girls (1997)

In the scene where Ashley Judd runs away from her attacker and falls into her aquarium he has moved to the bottom of the stairs - there is no way he would have been able to move that full fish tank. It looked to be about a 30 gallon tank - it would weigh about 400 pounds with the stand and even if he slid it with some superhuman strength, glass tanks are notorious for shattering when you move them full. Plus it would've made enough noise to wake the dead - no way she wouldn't have heard it.

The Lady Vanishes (1938)

When Iris Henderson and her two friends arrive at the hotel, Iris orders dinner and asks that it be sent up to "our" room. The waiter arrives when the three are changing. But later, when it's time for bed, Iris says good night to her friends, who leave her alone in the room (as she must be for the sake of subsequent developments).

Live Free or Die Hard (2007)

Since they took down the telephone network, it would have been impossible for Justin Long to even be speaking to the emergency response woman for the car, much less send a signal to start the car up.

The Lost World: Jurassic Park (1997)

Near the end of the movie, Peter Ludlow (the snivelling nephew of John Hammond who wants to create Jurassic Park in San Diego) is addressing company stockholders as they wait for the cargo ship to arrive. He says something to the effect of: "I'd like to thank you all for being intrepid enough to show up in the wee small hours of the morning." Those last six words, and the color of the sky make it seem like it is four or five in the morning at the latest. For that early, San Diego is a busy town. The buses are running, business men are out, video rental stores are open (and with plenty of customers), and generally a lot of people are out to run away from the T-Rex. I have to imagine that the mass of people running in terror (even though it is early in the morning) were put in as an homage to old monster movies. Same thing could be said for the Japanese business men. (01:38:10)

Minority Report (2002)

When Witwer invites Burgess over to discuss the problem of Anne Lively's murder, he gives Burgess Anderton's gun saying "We recovered that from Leo Crowe's hotel room", yet making no mention of why he is showing the gun. It makes no sense why he would bring the gun or give the gun to Burgess seeing as he would have to remove it from the evidence of the murder. There was no important evidence regarding the gun he would need to show Burgess and only seems to serve the plot (as Burgess uses the gun to kill Witwer at the end and the blame goes on Anderton). What complicates the matter further is that Witwer knows someone in the Pre-crime division was behind Anne Lively's murder, so to give a person who could very likely be involved in the murder a loaded gun seems a little risky and unnecessary. (01:45:50)

It's good to know that in the future we will be able to simply walk inside a car factory (without anybody working, neither employees, security people, or an automated protection system), get inside a brand new car and just drive away...

Mission: Impossible - Ghost Protocol (2011)

When Ethan meets the Secretary in the car, he tells him that Hendricks was seen leaving the Kremlin with the nuclear launch device and deduces that he is Cobalt. The Secretary then gives Ethan the flash drive containing his mission, which Ethan reads on the train. Ethan then tells the rest of the team that - according to the mission - IMF believes that Hendricks is Cobalt and was seen leaving the Kremlin with the launch device - hence why he needs to buy the launch codes from Moreau. How could IMF have known about this information to put it on the drive, given that Ethan just told the Secretary in the car?

National Treasure: Book of Secrets (2007)

In order for the treasure trail to be followed both desks would need to have existed in 1865 when the code was deciphered.

However HMS Resolute wasn't broken up and made into desks until 1879.

On the Line (2001)

When the Chicago Post first runs the story on Kevin, there is a picture of him on the front page, next to the headline. So anyone who was following the story would have known what he looked like, which would make it impossible for Kevin's friends to get away with pretending to be him.

The Parent Trap (1998)

The parents meet and get married on the QE II and then we jump to the girls getting to camp 11 years and nine months later. We learn their 12th birthdays are on October 11, so at the time of the camp (which must be around July/August) they are 11 years and around 9 months old. They should only be 11, given it takes 9 months to grow a baby, but instead they're nearly 12.

Poseidon (2006)

When the ship has turned on its side for the brief moment, it cuts to inside the ship where a hallway explodes, causing the ship to submerge. The only problem is the people are standing on the ceiling, but if the ship's on its side, they'd be on the wall, not ceiling.

The Purge: Election Year (2016)

When the security guy goes inside the secret hole, there is no way he'd have been able to cover the rug. When the other guys come in the rug is covering the hole.

Raiders of the Lost Ark (1981)

When Indy and Sallah visit the gentleman who translates the staff headpiece for them we hear the staff should be "six cadams high." Indy replies, "About 72 inches." Then, turning the headpiece over, "Wait - take back one cadam to honor the Hebrew God whose ark this is." It's definitely referring to the staff length - Indy says afterwards "Their staff is too long." So, about five feet now, right? But, when Indy goes to the map room the staff is much taller than him. If the staff is about five feet high, Indy would be around three feet tall. (00:48:25 - 00:53:05)

Robocop 3 (1993)

The opaque red lined map that Otomo retrieves from his first fight is ridiculous. Why would people who know where the hidden base is be carrying around a map on them (which shows a route so basic that they'd have to be brain-dead not to be able to remember it anyway) just so that conveniently one of their enemies can get it?

Rogue One: A Star Wars Story (2016)

When the inspection team goes into the Rogue One shuttle and then the Rebel team comes out of the shuttle in the inspection team's disguise, no one near the landing pad or in the building notices that two stormtroopers have disappeared from the group, the Imperial Officer has grown a beard in less than 5 minutes, and an Imperial Droid has come into the group.

Shrek Forever After (2010)

In the second Shrek movie, we find out that Fairy Godmother and the King had a deal that Prince Charming would save Princess Fiona from the keep, hence becoming her true love and breaking the curse. In the fourth movie, we start with Rumple monologuing about how he almost had the Kingdom by signing a deal with the King. Why would the King be so desperate to try and reverse the curse by signing a deal when he knows he has a prior attempt through Prince Charming, assuming it would take the same time for the messenger to return with news about Charming and Fiona either way?

Snakes on a Plane (2006)

The snakes escape from the locked box stored in the cargo hold when a small explosive bolt detonates and opens the lid. Post 9/11 all luggage placed in the cargo hold of an airliner would be tested for explosives, and anything larger than half a match head would be detected. The chances of getting an explosive bolt on board - nil. None whatever. You can also think of it this way - if the bad guys could somehow smuggle explosives on board, why bother with such an elaborate and flawed plan as letting snakes loose on the plane? Why not just smuggle a bomb on board? Pan Am 103 - the so-called Lockerbie flight - was brought down with a bomb that fit inside a small cassette player.

Spy Kids 3-D: Game Over (2003)

The Toymaker throws that toy bird at the hippie version of himself. The toy goes through him because he is a hologram. Later, he pushes the soldier version of himself at the screen making it crack. How could he if the three others are holograms?

Star Trek II: The Wrath of Khan (1982)

Why doesn't Reliant know that Khan is exiled here? The Federation is so terrified and opposed to genetic engineering that it's still illegal 300 years after Khan. So why is there no warning along with the data on the Ceti Alpha system? Kirk logged what happened with Khan and his solution of marooning him. Starships use nav data to navigate star systems. Ceti Alpha 6 exploded, yet the helmsman or computer never noticed that there is one less planet than there was when Kirk was there? There is no debris from the explosion? Ceti Alpha 5 is the exact same size and was conveniently blown into the exact same orbit as Ceti Alpha 6 used to have? So there is nothing whatsoever to make the crew even suspect that it's not 6? Enterprise would have to have scanned the planets in the system to know that one was habitable for Khan. Did Ceti Alpha 6's destruction somehow magically turn Ceti Alpha 5 into its exact duplicate? If Starfleet ships have been there to map after Ceti Alpha 6 exploded, none of them bothered to check on the exiles? Pretty callous for Starfleet, don't you think? With the technology and amounts of information available to Starfleet vessels, there is NO logical reason for the Reliant to think that this planet is Ceti Alpha 6. Finally, would the Federation be willing to test a device whose exact effects will be unknown on a planet so close to another inhabited one? (00:21:00)

The Sum of All Fears (2002)

When the President of the United States attends a public gathering (such as the SuperBowl) the level of security is extremely high. So why wasn't Mason's delivery on the day of the game checked for explosive devices?

Terminator 3: Rise of the Machines (2003)

The T-X did not hear Catherine in the Animal Hospital when she was only a few feet away and breathing loudly. Considering the scope of some of her technology, one would assume she would easily find her. (00:22:20)

Toy Story (1995)

The spaces in the lattice used as hand holds in the blue plastic crate in which Woody is trapped are easily large enough for him to squeeze through. He could have escaped without too much trouble.

Ultraviolet (2006)

Where did Cross get the blood on his hands? The gloves were clean of blood after he looked at the teeth and removed the gloves, so where did it come from?

Urban Legend (1998)

During the end the murderer is thrown out the front window of the building. The students leave the building through the front door, but yet there is no body, and that doesn't seem to bother them!

Westworld (1973)

There is a barely credible explanation for the fact that a guest cannot be injured or killed by being shot in Westworld, but what about the vicious fistfight we see in the bar? People are injured or killed in bar brawls all the time, and this once was incredibly violent. How do they prevent guests from being injured or killed by the cutting and stabbing weapons we see in Medieval and Roman World? Guests are supposed to fight each other, not just robots - they cannot be 'programmed' to lose! Delos is going be sued into bankruptcy within a week of the first guest arriving. Quite apart from the legal position, think about the bad publicity! Who is going to pay the huge fees demanded by the parks owners when the media is constantly reporting on the guests who wound up dead or with life changing injuries?

X-Men 2 (2003)

When the Drakes (Bobby's family) arrive home they are acting quite naturally, until they find Wolverine there and get a start. Later on we see that they had parked their van in the driveway right behind Cyclops' car, which Logan and company had borrowed and parked there. Wouldn't they, seeing a strange car in their driveway, be suspicious or at least enter their house asking "Bobby, are you home?" (00:52:45 - 00:59:15)

You Only Live Twice (1967)

The ferocious battle in the crater ends instantly when Bond blows up the space ship. Why? Aren't Blofeld's men still going to try to defend themselves? How do they know Bond has succeeded in his mission? They can't see the control room, let alone the television sets.

REVEALING MISTAKES

Anything which gives away filming techniques, such as stunt wires being visible, or glass smashing before anyone goes through it.

American Pie 2 (2001)

When Jim's Dad walks in on him and the girl having 'goodbye sex', Jim scrambles around trying to cover himself. At one point, as he's going from the floor to the bed, you can see the string bikini or whatever he's wearing so that he doesn't accidentally expose himself. (00:03:20)

Universal Pictures

Beverly Hills Cop (1984)

In the scene where Axel throws the art dealer's henchman onto the buffet table, if you watch carefully (or use slow-mo) you can see the stunt double pulling off that manoeuvre. There is also a stunt double being thrown over the table.

Bugsy Malone (1976)

When Tallulah and the girls are acting in the Fat Sam's Grand-slam song look at Tallulah as they sing the 'Ra da da da da da' bit. She looks straight into the camera.

Cabin Fever (2002)

When Bert is running in the woods, away from the local guys, he rubs blood on a tree to make them believe he ran a certain way. Look close, the tree already has red tint on it probably from previous takes that didn't wash off. (01:04:35)

Casino Royale (2006)

During the scene at the restaurant in Montenegro (actually filmed in the Czech Republic) you see a payphone with a Czech Telecom logo on it (itself a piece of history as these are all now rebranded O2). (01:57:50)

Charlie's Angels (2000)

When the Angels are picking through the wreckage of their headquarters, look at the only remaining wall - it's the thinnest wall you'll ever see. (01:02:20)

Christmas with the Kranks (2004)

When Vic Frohmeyer excitedly tells the kids that Mr. Krank is putting up his frosty, the kids turn their attention away from their video game and get up to leave, but the video game continues to be played, indicating the video on the screen is a recording. (00:59:20)

Die Another Day (2002)

When Bond is in the car following the goons heading into the facility, it shows the techie guy scan a card and then swipe it to open a door. Before he swipes it, the door is already opening. (01:13:15)

MGM Pictures

Dracula 2000 (2000)

During the ceiling sex scene, Lucy's hair lays flat against the ceiling with no effects of gravity while Dracula's hair hangs towards the floor fully under the proper force of gravity. (00:57:45)

The Fast and the Furious: Tokyo Drift (2006)

In the disco scene, the DJ is playing music, but the Pioneer decks and the DJ Mixer are not even turned on, as no lights are showing.

Freddy Vs. Jason (2003)

In the fight scene at the pier, after Freddy and Jason get thrown into the air by the carriage that smacks into them, they land on the pier in sort of slow motion. Watch Jason's left knee as he lands, you can see a kneepad.

Frozen (2013)

When Anna and Hans are dancing in front of the lighthouse, we don't see the shadow of the railing or the ground they're standing on.

Ghost (1990)

When Carl is being dragged away by the demons, you can see the cable line that he's attached to. May be fixed on DVD.

Gladiator (2000)

As Maximus approached his home after he should have been killed, the grain fields clearly show marks which are only caused by a tractor during crop spraying. (00:42:00)

Glory (1989)

When the 54th Mass. marches past a liberated plantation some black children wave them on. One of them is wearing a digital wristwatch.

Glory
Digital wristwatch during U.S. Civil War

TriStar

Halloween II (1981)

When Loomis shoots the marshal's window out, when he makes a u-turn you can see the tire marks on the road and dirt from previous takes.

Harry Potter and the Chamber of Secrets (2002)

When Ron is on all fours beginning to cough up slugs, Harry says "Let's take him to Hagrid's". Hermione mouths the lines with him. (00:39:43)

High School Musical (2006)

When Troy says "I'll sing with her," Ms. Darbus turns around "in response" to his voice before he even says anything.

Home Alone (1990)

Whenever Marv is outside walking in the snow in his bare feet you can tell that the feet aren't real.

Hostel (2005)

Before Paxton is hit with the 3 prong instrument, you can see the bloody holes already on his shirt. (01:01:20)

Indiana Jones and The Last Crusade (1989)

When Indy has just climbed the stairs in the library and is leaning over the rail to look at the X below, directly behind him is one of the worst props I've ever seen - a flat fake book case. (00:29:00)

Paramount Pictures

Jaws (1975)

When the shark bursts through the window of the cabin, in each of the shots facing Brody, including when he shoves the air tank into the shark's mouth, the glistening water is visible in the window's reflection behind Brody. The shark's reflection is never seen behind Brody, despite the shark's massive size in the small cabin. Bruce must have had the day off during Roy Scheider's takes. (01:58:00)

Jeepers Creepers (2001)

When the demon breaks into the jail and the cop is standing behind him. When the camera turns back on to the demon, if you look close you can see the zipper in the left hand side of the demon's suit. (01:08:45)

The League of Extraordinary Gentlemen (2003)

Mr Hyde makes no bubbles when growling underwater. (01:11:30)

Legally Blonde (2001)

When Elle is talking to Paulette on the cell phone, while waiting for the water, the woman before her goes to the water fountain, and you see her. She doesn't drink any water. She just puts her mouth next to the fountain. It is extremely obvious.

Liar Liar (1997)

When Fletcher is beating himself up he goes into a stall and squishes his head with a toilet seat. You can see that the white part underneath is made out of foam because it keeps squashing down.

The Lord of the Rings: The Fellowship of the Ring (2001)

After the battle with the cave Troll, Aragorn rushes over to injured Frodo and brushes past some big rocks that wobble, showing that they are lightweight and not real. (00:32:15)

The Man with the Golden Gun (1974)

During the fight scene in the belly dancer's room, Bond spins the bald guy around to avoid being hit by a chair. When the bald guy gets hit in the back with the chair, you can see a large rectangle of padding under his jacket.

The Matrix Reloaded (2003)

During the freeway scene, if you look closely, you will notice that some of the trucks have no axles. Most obvious is the second one the camera goes under when following Trinity on the bike.

Warner Bros. Pictures

Men in Black (1997)

When Will Smith throws a rock at the escaping Edgar alien, if you watch the rock after it hits the alien, it disappears after hitting the ground. (01:23:20)

Midway (1976)

In the final scene where Fonda and Holbrook are looking over the carrier at the crowds on the dock you can see that only the first rows of people are dressed in period clothes, the rest of the crowd are dressed as they would have been in 1976 when the film was made.

Miss Congeniality (2000)

At the pageant, Cheryl performs with the flaming batons and she tosses a baton into the air. Cheryl's reflection is seen on the stage floor but the baton's is not because she really tosses nothing, this particular baton is entirely CG. Also, in some shots when her reflection and the reflections of bulbs, etc, is seen on the stage floor, the reflections of the flames are not. The flames were real in some shots and digitally augmented in others. (01:26:55)

In the opening close-up of adult Gracie, her eyes are looking over the faux book entitled 'Essentials of Russian Grammar'. There is a camera lens through the binding of the book in the center of the letter 'o' in the word 'of'. In the next close-up and semi close-up of Gracie, the camera lens is not in the binding, it's just the title of the book. One giveaway, the diameter of the lens in the first shot is greater than the diameter of the 'o' in the subsequent shots. (00:02:20)

Mission: Impossible - Rogue Nation (2015)

When Benji imagines putting on a mask of an agent he plans to impersonate, when the camera pans around to first show the mirror, the mirror Benji's hands are further up on his face than the reflection, and the mirror Benji's hands move down his face slightly before the reflection starts to move them. Also, the mole that Ethan has on his left cheek isn't reversed in the mirror image. The "mirror" was actually a hole in the wall between two identical sets (one mirrored), with Simon Pegg and a Tom Cruise double in the foreground, and the mask actor and Tom Cruise in the background "mirror" set. (00:57:20)

Moulin Rouge (2001)

There is a shot where the point of view of the camera is looking down at Christian and Toulouse from the opening in his ceiling. You can see John Leguizamo's legs behind him and that he is kneeling down. (00:06:00)

20th Century Fox

The Mummy Returns (2001)

In the visions of Nefertiri scene where Nefertiri is fighting Anck-su-Namun back in ancient Egypt, Evie (Nefertiri) gets knocked to the floor and when she lifts her mask up you can see on her right index finger is a band aid/plaster. Did they have plasters back in ancient times? (01:07:49)

The Mummy Returns

Modern plaster/band-aid visible

Universal Pictures

In the British Museum after O'Connell frees Evie from being sacrificed, they both shoot at glass containers filled with alcohol and formaldehyde. Right before they explode, you can see protective masks very clearly on the guards that were standing in front of them. (00:39:51)

The Mummy Returns
Protective masks visible

Universal Pictures

Never Been Kissed (1999)

When Rob is in the Cafeteria eating all the coleslaw, he yells "I'm the coleslaw king of the world!" there is a girl in the background who mouths it as he is saying it. (00:50:00)

The Parent Trap (1998)

When Hallie trashes Annie's cabin and the huge water balloon is about to fall on Annie's head, the camera is at a downward view and Annie clearly steps into the trail of the balloon instead of jumping away. (00:18:05)

Passenger 57 (1992)

When the terrorists drop the dead body out the aircraft door, look closely at the aeroplane just beneath the door, you can see the reflection of the mat the stuntman lands on, as well as the spotters around it.

The Princess Bride (1987)

When Inigo and Westley are duelling, they are making athletic jumps. One does it after the other and when they land you can see the mat wrinkle under the "dirt" on the ground.

Red 2 (2013)

When Han shoots at Bruce Willis and the others with the Gatling gun, we see cartridges on the ground. You can tell that they are all blanks. The tip is jagged and has been closed - live ammo just has an open hole where the bullet was.

The Rocky Horror Picture Show (1975)

When Dr. Scott is being pulled through the castle by the Triple Contact Electro-Magnet, you can see the cable and the cut in the carpet, that the cable runs under, pulling his wheelchair at the top of one of the staircases. (01:01:00)

20th Century Fox

When Rocky lifts Frank-N-Furter's body Rocky is barefoot, wearing only the stockings. When Rocky is climbing the RKO tower, carrying his creator, evidently Rocky is wearing a type of thin shoes *under* his stockings. The stunt double did this as a safety precaution. (01:30:35)

The Rocky Horror Picture Show
Bare stocking feet suddenly acquire shoes

The saxophone Eddie plays in "Hot Patootie" has no reed. (00:43:10)

Romeo and Juliet (1968)

When you see the first shot of the dead Mercutio, he's still breathing.

Scream (1996)

As Drew Barrymore is running from the killer outside he stabs her. If you look closely it is very easy to tell it is a rubber knife, because you see it bend off of her. (00:10:20)

Snake Eyes (1998)

After the sniper is shot he falls through the wall. Look at his silencer when he hits the ground - it bends where it attaches to the muzzle. A real metal silencer wouldn't do that. (00:41:25)

Speed (1994)

After the first bus explosion when Jack answers the phone, he looks at his watch, which shows 8:05 a.m. If you look closely the watch is on alarm, not regular time. (00:29:05)

Speed
Checks watch but shows alarm not real time

20th Century Fox

Star Wars (1977)

In the Death Star corridor leading to the Millennium Falcon, just before Han says "Didn't we just leave this party?" you can see Carrie Fisher and Mark Hamill's shadows on the wall as they await their cue to run in. (01:31:30)

When an Imperial Officer is running down the tunnel in the Detention Block towards Han, Luke and Chewbacca, Han clearly shoots the top-left hand corner of the tunnel and the Imperial Officer falls down the stairs as if he shot him. (01:14:55)

Star Wars
Blast hits wall yet officer falls

20th Century Fox

Just before Lord Vader appears the first time (on the boarded consular ship, through the breached door), there is a Storm-trooper checking another trooper apparently dead on the floor (he's lifting the dead one's head). Then Vader enters, and the Stormtrooper quickly straightens up, dropping the head. It turns out the "dead" Stormtrooper was actually alive, however, because he carefully lowers his own head to the floor. (00:04:30)

Star Wars: Episode II - Attack of the Clones (2002)

When Padme and Anakin enter the droid production centre, there is a shot of them going through a large door. Though they both crouch slightly, Anakin's head passes through the door. (01:36:35)

Star Wars: Episode III - Revenge of the Sith (2005)

When Yoda knocks Darth Sidious backwards over his chair, you can see the stuntman's hand. Sidious's hands are old and his nails are dark around the cuticles, but the hand during the flip is perfectly healthy and a different size. (01:45:35)

Thunderball (1965)

In the scene where Bond is trapped in Largo's shark-infested pool, he uses his mini air tank to breathe. In most of the subsequent shots, look closely at the actor's face: it looks a lot more like a stuntman than Sean Connery. (01:20:20)

Troy (2004)

When the spear handle is protruding from Hector's shoulder, the area of the armor around the circular wound is clearly visible and it is in perfect condition. There is no tear in the armor whatsoever, around the wood, which would have been necessary to allow the wide spear tip to penetrate the armor and actually enter Hector's body as it did. (02:01:20)

During their fight in front of Troy's wall, Ajax shoves his weapon into Hector's face, causing Hector to fall back. In the next shot looking up, as Hector hits the ground, part of the wall is gone. There is even a bit of the crew's scaffold, visible behind the edge of the 'stone'. This particular piece of wall was never built as part of the actual set, so when it appears onscreen it is always CG, though in this shot the composite people did not complete it and at this precise angle it should be there. When the bodies are being collected (at the end of this battle), there is a good view of the wall intact. (01:20:00)

You Only Live Twice (1967)

In the car chase, the girl keeps the steering wheel straight all the time (in the shot from inside the car), although the street is not straight at all.

During the car chase scene, if you watch the speedometer on the car, it never rises above zero. That and the obviously poor image quality of the "road" in front of them shows that they were using projected film in front of the car.

Zulu (1964)

When Mr Witt rides out of the Zulu camp in a 2 horse cart at the beginning of the movie, just before it exits, you can see it's a stunt double at the reins.

AUDIO PROBLEMS

Anything related to sound, such as echoes in the wrong place, or speech not matching lip movements.

Ace Ventura: Pet Detective (1994)

Right after the "Mission Impossible" theme when he gets into the shark tank room, he slams the door, but you hear the door slam before it actually slams all the way shut.

Alex and Emma (2003)

When Alex is trying to talk Emma into staying as they walk down the stairs in Alex's apartment building, Alex mouths something completely different from what is being said.

Annie (1982)

When Punjab is making the plant move by magic in front of Annie (just before Grace walks in and tells Annie that she is going to Washington DC to meet the President), he lands it on a table, and she says "Wow", but her lips don't move - she just smiles at him.

Austin Powers: The Spy Who Shagged Me (1999)

Towards the end, when Felicity Shagwell is captured in that glass tube, there's a shot of the entire room and she is yelling for Austin Powers but her lips aren't moving.

The Aviator (2004)

Towards the end of the scene where L.B. Mayer is dismissing Howard's request for some cameras, the audio does not match at all with the way his lips are moving.

The Borrowers (1997)

When Spiller throws the rope in the milk bottle trying to pull Peagreen out, you can hear him straining and grunting to keep a hold of it but his face and mouth are both relaxed.

Camp Rock (2008)

In the Final Jam scene, when Mitchie is singing the lines "Every day and every night, it's all we want to do in life," Caitlin and Shane can be seen mouthing "We rock, we rock, we rock," in the background, but it is not actually being sung. (01:32:05)

Carry On Cabby (1963)

When Sarge is giving instructions to Allbright over the taxi radio Allbright replies "I don't know what the union's going to say about all this" to which Sarge replies "**** the union". His mouth doesn't open while the noise sounds to cover up his swear word.

Catch Me If You Can (2002)

When Handratty is in France telling Frank that there are 20 officers outside, you can see when the camera turns to Frank, Handratty's mouth is still moving despite the fact that he is not talking. (01:55:40)

Con Air (1997)

There is a scene where Johnny 23 is on the tower and he sees all of those cars coming. He runs, and while he's running he yells "holy shi*". His mouth didn't move at all. (01:12:20)

The Dark Knight (2008)

In the scene where Alfred is stitching up Bruce, Bruce says "I wanted to inspire people." As he says "people" the shot changes and his lips aren't moving, but the audio track continues.

Darkness Falls (2003)

When Caitlin and Michael are under the bed, Caitlin says "Okay, maybe we should stay under the bed," but her mouth doesn't move.

Days of Thunder (1990)

In one scene Tom Cruise's accelerator gets stuck - you see him pounding on the accelerator while telling his crew chief Harry Hog "the accelerator is stuck" but Tom Cruise's mouth never moves when he speaks.

Die Hard 2 (1990)

When the terrorist at the church goes inside and asks "where's Cochrane", the other replies "he didn't make it." His mouth isn't moving.

Dr. No (1962)

When the powerboat shoots at the island, afterward, when the guy with the speakerphone tells them that he would be back later on, he then turns to the driver and tells him to move on, but when he says that, it sounds as though he's still talking in the microphone even thought the microphone is at his side.

The Five Heartbeats (1991)

When Eddie runs in and starts singing "I Got Nothing But Love" the song is playing in the background and the lyrics can be heard ahead of him actually singing them.

Friday the 13th (1980)

In the beginning, Claudette and the other counsellors are all singing. When they get closer you can see that Claudette is playing the guitar, then she stops, but the guitar playing and singing still continues. (00:02:10)

The Godfather (1972)

When Carlo gets strangled in the car and kicks the windshield the sound of breaking glass can be heard before it actually happens. (02:41:05)

The Goonies (1985)

When Data turns on the 'bully blinders', the others are blinded by the light. As they follow him we hear Mouth shout, "Who is that? Oh Stef that's you, watch out! Data!" his mouth is not in sync with any of it. (00:48:20)

The Great Dictator (1940)

When Hynkel refers to the peace treaty and says "I'll sign it," you can hear the sound quality change abruptly, and when Hynkel is saying "Napoloni the grosse peanut, the cheesy ravioli," his lips are not in sync.

Halloween III: Season of the Witch (1982)

During the scene where Dr. Challis goes to visit his two kids, they put on their Halloween masks and his little son says "Let's watch TV." He goes to turn the knob to turn on the TV and a split second BEFORE he turns it, we can hear the intro of the commercial on the television.

Hang 'Em High (1968)

At the start of the movie, when Clint Eastwood says "You're making a mistake," his lips don't seem to be moving.

Harry Potter and the Chamber of Secrets (2002)

Hermione takes her wand out in the shot facing her, Harry and Ron, and Hermione's mouth begins to shout the "I" in "Immobulus!" though no sound is heard. It is in the next close-up that she dramatically shouts out the entire word, "Immobulus!" (00:37:40)

High School Musical (2006)

In "What I've Been Looking For", when Sharpay sings the last verse the first time around, listen closely as Ryan takes away the microphone. Her voice remains the same volume, and does not get any quieter as Ryan pulls away the microphone.

High School Musical 2 (2007)

When Troy and Gabriella are singing "Everyday," Troy sings with his microphone away from his mouth numerous times during the scene, yet he is still heard just as well, and not at a lower level, like he should be. (Within the context of the film, this is sung live on stage and is not implied to be pre-recorded.)

I Am Legend (2007)

During the scene where he is hitting golf balls off of the ship, he is hitting an iron. For anyone who plays golf, the sound that goes along with this is that of a driver or some type of fairway metal.

I Know Who Killed Me (2007)

When Dakota and Jerrod start having sex, Aubrey's mother can hear Jerrod's moans through the ceiling. But up until they *really* start getting into the act, the moans that Susan is hearing don't match the shots in the bedroom.

I Still Know What You Did Last Summer (1998)

When Julie wakes up and turns the lamp on, and it goes off, Julie says "Shit" but her mouth says "ouch." (00:08:25)

Iron Monkey (1993)

When Miss Orchid is making dinner for Wong Kei-Ying, she turns to him and tells him about a special chili that is made. When she turns back to her cooking, she tells him how hot it is but her mouth doesn't move.

The Island (2005)

When Lincoln 6 Echo is watching the the surgeons kill the other 'product' after giving birth, her heart monitor flat-lines well before the sound does. It beeps about 4 times before the shot changes to a closeup of the flat-line. (00:34:50)

Kingdom of Heaven (2005)

When the Christian army is defeated after chasing Saladin across the desert, many vultures are flying over the battlefield. However, the sound is that of a flock of whooping cranes.

Lemony Snicket's A Series of Unfortunate Events (2004)

When Aunt Josephine says, " Watch the chandelier, if it falls it will impale you." she turns to face the camera about when she says "impale" and her lips aren't moving. (00:50:05)

The Lion King II: Simba's Pride (1998)

In the scene where Simba is being attacked by Zira and the other outlanders, he rolls down a small cliff. Zira then says, "Yes, we've got him", but if you watch her mouth she is actually laughing and her mouth isn't moving at all.

Live and Let Die (1973)

Before Bond and Solitaire gets into Kanaga's den in the end of the movie, we see two guards running. However there are only footsteps from one person.

Live Free or Die Hard (2007)

During the final chase scene when McClane takes control of the semi truck, you can hear the truck continuing to shift gears even though McClane is not completely in the driver's seat and nowhere close to the clutch or shifter.

Look Who's Talking (1989)

When James is rushing Mollie to the hospital, the camera is down the road from the taxi. James is saying something like, "You should do Lamaze breathing. It helped my sister," yet his mouth is not moving.

The Lord of the Rings: The Two Towers (2002)

When the Ents are attacking Isengard, just after the river has been released. Merry calls to Pippin "hold on!", but if you look at his lips, he says "Hang on!" The lip-syncing doesn't match. (02:35:25)

Mallrats (1995)

In the DVD version, before Brodie says to TS, "I suddenly want something very bad to happen to you," you can hear Kevin Smith or someone say "Action."

The Matrix (1999)

In the lobby shootout, you can see two soldiers firing at Neo just before he does his cartwheel. Both of their weapons have the sound of an M16, but the first soldier is actually holding a pump action shotgun. You can even see the shell being ejected.

The Other Boleyn Girl (2008)

In the scene where Mary is leaving court and you see Henry riding a horse with Anne on the back, you can hear a siren go off twice. (01:05:30 - 01:06:10)

Pee-wee's Big Adventure (1985)

The carts the guards are chasing Pee-Wee in are electric, which we see when they first get to them and have to unplug them. However throughout the entire chase scene we distinctly hear gas engine sound effects. (01:12:30)

The Phantom of the Opera (2004)

During the end of "Prima Donna" when everyone sings "Light up the stage." you can see some actors and actresses singing the word "light" but you don't actually hear it until a few seconds later.

The Room (2003)

Much of Johnny's dialog is dubbed in throughout the film, with his lips and dialog not quite matching. (This is due to actor/director Tommy Wiseau's thick accent making the original dialogue sometimes hard to understand).

Scooby-Doo and the Cyber Chase (2001)

On the first level of the video game, after Velma brings up what she remembers what Eric said about the Scooby snacks in the game, you hear Daphne talking but you see Velma's lips moving. (00:01:00)

The Score (2001)

Nick uses the periscope camera through the grate of the basement floor. There is first a shot of the camera poking out and that is followed by a shot of a hand-held screen accompanied by a camera zoom sound as he zooms. Generally the zoom sound would come from the camera itself rather than the screen and a camera that size is not likely to make a electronic zoom sound of that amplitude. (00:43:20)

Selena (1997)

In the scene where Selena opens her boutique, she introduces Yolanda Saldivar. The camera zooms in on Yolanda, but you can still see that Selena's mouth doesn't move when she says, "She's my fan club president."

Sky High (2005)

When Will meets Layla at the bus stop he says to her "You're not going to believe what happened to me last night," however his mouth continues to move after he says this. (00:59:00)

The Sound of Music (1965)

During the bedroom storm scene singing "My Favorite Things", Marta is sitting next to Fräulein Maria and she gets wrapped up in the moment of Maria singing and mouths "feel so bad" - she's not supposed to be singing.

Speed (1994)

As Payne cries "My Money!" when shooting at Jack, who is on top of the train, his mouth doesn't match what he is saying. (01:38:50)

Spider-Man (2002)

When Mary Jane is about to fall from the balcony and the Green Goblin appears in front of her, we hear him say, "Hello, my dear," but his mouth is not in sync with those words. (01:07:40)

Stand By Me (1986)

At the beginning when Vern comes to the tree house to share his exciting news, when he is climbing up to get inside his lips do not match what he is saying. (00:03:40)

Star Wars: Episode I - The Phantom Menace (1999)

After Anakin has won the Podrace, he yells, "Mum, I did it! Yeah!", but the words don't quite fit his actual lip movement. (01:07:00)

Surf's Up (2007)

At the scene where Mikey asks the elder penguin if anyone surfs in Shiverpool, when he says,"You know you're standing on thin ice," his beak never moves.

Titanic (1997)

When Rose is talking to Thomas Andrews, telling him to tell her the truth about what has happened, listen to the voices in the background. At one point in the scene you can hear someone saying "Yes madam, please put it on immediately", then some-one laughs. Right at the end of the scene, the same line can be heard in exactly the same tone of voice, followed by the laugh - it's obviously a loop. Although some tracks in the mix of the soundtrack do not loop at that moment, the track with the mentioned sentence does. (01:47:30)

When the Captain is watching the overturned boat trying to be launched, there is a crew member working on the davit, causing it to make a rapid clicking noise. But soon after the noise stops, the crewmember is still turning. (02:29:15)

Transformers (2007)

Before they leave for Mission City, Lennox tells Keller, "Sir, you gotta figure out some way to get word out..." Then in the next shot, as Lennox shouts, "Let's move!" his mouth stays open - not forming the "m" with his lips to produce the word "move", which we hear very clearly (it looks as if he really said, "Let's go!"). Changes in dialogue are done during ADR and often are not in sync with mouth movements seen onscreen. (01:45:45)

Watchmen (2009)

During the battle in Adrian Veidt's lair he catches a bullet. He pulls the slug from his palm but as he drops the slug we hear the sound of a spent shell casing hitting the floor (empty brass) not the heavy lead bullet.

Wedding Crashers (2005)

In the scene where Todd and Jeremy are in the bedroom together and Todd is lying on top of Jeremy asking to play "tummysticks", - right before Sen Clary is about to come in and Jeremy begins to panic, watch Jeremy as he's lying on the bed talking. You hear him say about three sentences, but see his mouth move for about one from the left side view of his mouth.

The World is Not Enough (1999)

When Bond arrives at the King Industries place where he meets Elektra King, watch the man he talks to when he gets out of his car. It is painfully obvious that the man's mouth is not in sync with what he is saying. Even worse, the voice is not even his. It is slightly higher-pitched than the man's real voice when he finally talks right.

You Only Live Twice (1967)

In the volcano's control room, there is a husky guy in red uniform whose only purpose is to open and close the crater. Every time he opens or closes the crater he says with a deep voice, "opening crater, closing crater." When Bond kills him with the rocket cigarette to open the crater and let the ninjas in, and the guards have subdued Bond, the guard in white uniform who closes the crater says, "closing crater," and you can hear that it's the dead husky guy's voice.

CHARACTER MISTAKES

Something a character wrongly states as fact, or spelling mistakes. Something more significant than a minor error anyone could make.

3 Idiots (2009)

Just after the birth of Mona's child, Farhan recollects "uss waqt agar Virus kehta kay mera pouta engineer.". In fact the child is not his "pouta" but his "nata"

The Abyss (1989)

When they're reviving Lindsey, Bud screams "fight" and slaps her. watch as she closes her eyes on the second slap while she is supposed to be dead.

Ace Ventura: Pet Detective (1994)

In the scene at Roger Podacter's condo building, you hear the reporter mention that he allegedly leaped to his death from his own 20th story balcony. As the camera pans down, you can see the flashlights and people up on his balcony doing the investigation. This is the 2nd from the top floor. If you count the floors as the camera moves down, there are more than 20 floors to this building. The number is actually closer to 30. Even though it is difficult to get an exact count of the floors, it is still possible to tell with 100% certainty that his unit was on a floor higher than 20.

Apocalypse Now (1979)

After Captain Willard walks through the front door of the burnt out French plantation dock there's a close-up of Chief Phillips at the wheel the boat. He turns around and looks right at Chef and says, "Lance". (01:56:40)

Awake (2007)

The endotracheal tube (breathing tube) was not secured to the patient. It is standard practice to secure this tube to the patient in order to keep it in place.

Back to the Future Part II (1989)

When Doc and Marty are driving on the Sky Way Doc says "damn this traffic," but in the reflection of the DeLorean's front window there are no cars.

Christmas with the Kranks (2004)

Towards the end of the movie when Tim Allen is on the roof and the fire squad is called. One of the firemen carrying the ladder accidentally hits a man in the head with it.

Common mistakes

In almost every film or TV show, if the villain actually bothered to kill the hero as soon as they met face to face instead of just talking about their plans, the villain would actually succeed in his or her plans. Instead, the villain letting the hero live becomes their real downfall.

Creed II (2018)

The commentator says "avalanche of power shots by Ivan Drago." Viktor is the one in the ring. Ivan is the father. If you have the subtitles turned on, it even says Viktor in the subtitles instead of the spoken name, Ivan. (00:55:45)

Crimson Tide (1995)

At the end of the movie, Ramsey and Hunter begin a conversation about Lippizaner horses. Ramsey says they are from Portugal, Hunter says they are from Spain. However, the Lippizaner horse's place of origin is believed to be in modern day Slovenia (though they are believed to have descended from Spain in the distant past). Lippizan is Slovenia's national symbol. Plus Lippizans are associated with the 'Spanish Riding school' but the 'Spanish Riding School' is situated in Vienna, Austria.

When Denzel is talking to the crew about upgrading to DEFCON 3, they say the last time was 32 1/2 years ago during the Cuban missile crisis of October 1962. The problem is that they both take place during October, meaning that the half year part is a mistake. (00:34:00)

Django Unchained (2012)

The check written by Sam Jackson says May 2, 1858. At this point in the movie, it should be 1859.

Fast & Furious 6 (2013)

Tej mentions that the BMWs they used were factory-line, ie. unmodified. Hobbs then says that they were twin-turbo V8s "spitting out 560 ponies". The BMW M5s they have are E60 models (2005-2010) powered by a naturally aspirated 5.0 liter V10, producing 507 horsepower. (00:38:30)

Fast Times at Ridgemont High (1982)

In history class, Mr. Hand tells the students that the Platt Amendment was an amendment to the U.S. Constitution passed in 1906. In fact, it was a rider attached to the Army Appropriations Act of 1901. (00:23:05)

Field of Dreams (1989)

Chick Gandil mispronounces Eddie Cicotte's name, calling him "Si-coty" instead of "See-cot."

Flight (2012)

When Whip is in hospital, a nurse comes in with the others but what she does with the IV is all wrong. First: she tosses the empty IV bag onto the floor - you never do that - and then she proceeds to tug continually on the base of another IV bag, trying to get the IV line out of the bag - this she does not succeed in doing.

Friday (1995)

When Craig gets the milk out of the fridge he takes it to the table and pours it on his cereal. He looks surprised when there isn't much in the carton. He would've known this from the weight of the carton when he first picked it up.

Ghost Rider (2007)

When Johnny Blaze plans on jumping the football field he says he is jumping field goal to field goal. The movie says multiple times he is jumping 300 feet. End zone to end zone is 300 feet. Field goal post to field goal post is 360 feet.

Good Morning, Vietnam (1987)

When Cronauer and Garlick get stuck in traffic with the Army trucks, Garlick asks the assembled troops to guess who is in the Jeep with him. One of the troops shouts "Mork". Robin Williams played Mork in *Mork & Mindy*, but not until 1978, well after the setting of this film.

The Great Debaters (2007)

The definition of Satyagraha that Wilson, the butler at Harvard, gives is partially correct. Wilson defines it as "truth and fairness." A quick look at Wikipedia defines Satyagraha as "holding the truth." The definition from the online Merriam-Webster dictionary could be loosely described as "persistence of truth." (01:38:30)

Hanover Street (1979)

Before they jump off the plane Halloran should at least have checked if Sellinger has his parachute strapped on properly, knowing that the other guy has absolutely no experience. (01:05:55)

Harry Potter and the Philosopher's Stone (2001)

When Wood is telling Harry the rules of Quidditch he says that if you catch the Snitch the game is over, which is true but then he also says that which ever seeker catches the snitch, their team wins, but that isn't true. Granted that the 150 extra points probably would give you the winning lead, but as JKR pointed out in the 4th book at the Quidditch World Cup, you can catch the Snitch but lose the match. And you'd think explaining the rules to a first-timer you would want to get it right. (01:05:40)

I Know Who Killed Me (2007)

The coroner examining Jennifer Toland's body reports that her fingers were cut off first, then the metacarpals (palm bones) were removed later. Given that when she is found her entire limb is missing up to her mid-forearm, how could he possibly tell not only that the missing part was not all removed at once, but which bits were cut off in which order?

In the Line of Fire (1993)

During the "heart attack prank" just before the paramedics get to Frank, Eastwood mistakenly opens his eye before the paramedics wake him.

Inglourious Basterds (2009)

Hicox salutes General Fenech, who returns the salute. But Fenech is bareheaded and therefore under British military protocol cannot salute. He would instead acknowledge the salute with a nod.

It's a Mad Mad Mad Mad World (1963)

When Spencer Tracy is talking to his wife and daughter on two separate telephones, he places the phones up against each other so mom and daughter can talk to each other. One phone should be upside down so it would be speaker to transmitter rather than speaker to speaker.

Johnny English (2003)

Sauvage declares that he is going to turn England into a prison, but the graphic he is displaying puts the prison walls around the entire island of Great Britain. (01:03:30)

Justice League: The Flashpoint Paradox (2013)

One of the top most taboo things for a super hero to do is reveal any aspect of another hero's identity to someone, especially a villain. But when Flash is trapped by the gray adhesive and the other Justice League members are about to take the villains away to disarm the bombs, Flash tells Green Lantern "Hal, go", calling Green Lantern by his first name right in front of Mirror Master. (00:08:05)

Law Abiding Citizen (2009)

Clyde enters his cell in the final scene, and is surprised to find that he has been found out. His secret tunnel, if we go according to the characteristics accredited to his character throughout the movie, is surprisingly without any alarms of any sort. Very strange if we are to believe he is as deadly as credited. He ends dying a very silly death.

Lethal Weapon 3 (1992)

The "MAC-10" machine pistol used by Darryl and Sergeant Murtough is actually a Cobray M11/9.

The Lost World (1960)

At the end, Professor Challenger misidentifies the dinosaur in the boiling water as a T-Rex. Its arms are too long, and it sports horns. It is much more likely a carnotaur. This area being a forte of his, I doubt Professor Challenger would make this mistake.

Love Actually (2003)

When Jamie is first speaking to Aurelia, he says "molto bueno", which the housekeeper woman tells him is Spanish. 'Molto' is actually Italian. (00:38:30)

Maximum Overdrive (1986)

When Curtis and Connie stop at the first gas station, the word diesel is misspelled as disel.

Midway (1976)

When the Japanese attack is imminent, a soldier loads the 50 caliber machine gun rounds into the box backwards, with the rounds facing the gunner.

Monster (2003)

When Selby goes out to meet friends, they talk about going to "Fun World" in Orlando. However, they did not actually visit "Fun World" they went to "Fun Spot" (look at the signs on the ferris wheel and behind the carousel). Fun Spot is located on international drive in Orlando where as "Fun World" is another amusement park. (01:07:55)

National Lampoon's Christmas Vacation (1989)

Clark has too many lights on his house causing the city to go dark. There is a scene where the power plant needs to boost their output. There is a close-up of a guy flipping the switch. Look at the way they spelled auxiliary - auxilliary. (00:37:54)

Warner Bros. Pictures

National Treasure (2004)

Nick states that Wall Street was originally a wall (correct) built to defend against the British (incorrect.) The original wall was a wooden palisade built in the 16th Century to defend the colonists against invading natives and to prevent livestock from wandering uptown.

Nativity! (2009)

When Mr Maddens is talking to the critic at the Mayor's reception, he calls him Alan. The character is actually called Patrick

Burns, Alan is the actor's name.

No Country For Old Men (2007)

When Moss is arguing with the border guard at the Eagle Pass international bridge, he claims that he is a veteran of the "12th Infantry Battalion." There has never been such a thing as the 12th Infantry Battalion in either the Army or the Marines. Rather, they are based on a structure of 3-4 battalions per numbered regiment (i.e., 1st Battalion, 3rd Infantry Regiment/2nd Battalion, 5th Marine Regiment, etc). The film takes this seriously, as the guard, a veteran himself, buys Moss' story.

Ocean's Eleven (1960)

In one scene, one of the people suggests that Danny Ocean should run for President, and the first plan of action was to repeal the "13th and 20th" Amendments to the constitution, allowing women to lose the vote and go back into slavery. The 20th Amendment has nothing to do with women's right of voting, that is the 19th Amendment. If the 20th Amendment were repealed, the President would again take office on March 4th in the year following the election.

Oliver (1968)

In the beginning of the film, Oliver has been brought by Mr. and Mrs. Bumble to the Governor's door after asking for more to eat. Mrs. Bumble then sings, "They'll lay the blame on the one who named him," and as Mr. Bumble is responding, "O-li-ver", look at Oliver. He is completely spacing out and not in character at all - staring off into the distance and flicking his tongue in and out of his mouth.

The Open House (2018)

When Logan tries to use both his and his mom's phones after her fingers were broken by the Man in Black, he throws them in disgust when he finds the SIM cards have been removed. However, every cell is capable of placing a 911 call regardless of whether a SIM card is present or not.

Prometheus (2012)

The ship travels approximately 35 light years, yet Vickers (Charlize Theron) comments they are half a billion miles from Earth. That would barely get them past Jupiter, much less another solar system.

The Quick and The Dead (1987)

When Vallian prepares to leave the homestead, McKaskell asks him how his chest wound was. Vallian was shot low on the right side, just above the gun-belt, and McKaskell, who removed the bullet, was quite aware of the location.

Rocky IV (1985)

When Rocky makes his speech after his fight with Drago, he says that it's better that one person fights another instead of a million fighting a million (a US USSR war). The Russian translator misinterprets his speech and says that this is better than a million dollars. You don't have to understand Russian (although I do) to hear the translator says million dollars to confirm this blunder of a mistake. (01:22:25)

See Spot Run (2001)

At the FBI facility, Agent 11's handler buckles the collar on the dog's neck. Later, when Gordon has put the collar on and tries to get it off, he's trying to pry it off. He just buckled it on not two minutes earlier. He's stupid, but not that stupid.

Sister Act (1992)

During the end credits, three of the magazine covers spell Whoopi's character's name as "Delores." Two of the covers spell it "Deloris," as do the credits.

Sixteen Candles (1984)

In the scene where Sam is filling out the confidential questionnaire, the word "confidential" is spelled "confidentail".

Sky Captain and the World of Tomorrow (2004)

After the robots first attack New York City, a series of newspapers is shown. One of the headlines in the French one reads "La Tour Eiffeil est détruite". The proper spelling is "Eiffel" (00:15:55)

The Sons of Katie Elder (1965)

The 4 brothers have just rode into town and are securing their horses. On the flag pole in the background the Texas flag is upside down. Note: The correct way is white flies on top and red on bottom.

Star Trek: First Contact (1996)

When Picard is explaining the Enterprise to Lily he states that it has 24 decks. Yet earlier on, a crewman had reported to Worf that the Borg had taken over "decks 26 up to 11".

Star Trek: Insurrection (1998)

When Will Riker comes to Troi's office and kisses her, Troi says that she has never kissed him with a beard before, but in the third season episode "Menage a Troi", Troi does in fact kiss a bearded Will Riker, while on leave at Betazed, in the Fifth season "The Outcast", and again in season six's "Man of The People." (00:26:45)

Step Brothers (2008)

When Brennan's brother is talking to Jack in the kitchen, he is holding a Heineken beer. However when he goes out in the tree house and shows the brothers his six pack, he claims he hasn't had a carb since 2000.

Street Fighter (1994)

When Guile promises to rescue the hostages while on camera with Bison he makes a point to mention Charlie by name to reassure him that he wasn't forgotten. Anybody who was in charge of a major recovery operation would know better than to mention a specific hostage that isn't already well known to the enemy because he just put a target on that hostage for further abuse. This was promptly shown in the following scene when Bison picked out Charlie to be transformed into a beast as a result of Guile identifying him as a personal friend.

Swimfan (2002)

Right before Madison shoots the 2 police officers they show a close-up of the gun in its holster. The holster is unbuttoned. No police officer would leave his gun holster unbuttoned, especially while sitting next to a felon.

Top Gun (1986)

In the opening scene is a paragraph describing why the Top Gun school was started. The word "insure" is used when the word should have been "ensure". They wanted to guarantee the U.S. had superior pilots, not take out an insurance policy.

The Towering Inferno (1974)

Just before the fire starts on the 81st floor, a man is shown telling an elderly couple that business offices only go as high as 80, and that 81-120 is exclusively residential. Not long after O'Hallorhan arrives, he asks Jernigan for a list of business tenants from 81-85, which Jernigan replies "most are yet to move in and those that have are not working at night". As said by the man earlier, these floors do not house business tenants, only residential. (00:12:05 - 00:43:45)

What A Girl Wants (2003)

In the scene where the photos of Daphne are flashing by, you see her in a photograph which was supposedly taken at the Chelsea Charity Auction. In the caption, "auction" is incorrectly spelled "aution."

White House Down (2013)

Towards the start, when Emily mentions that the presidential limo is based on a Cadillac CTS, she is wrong. The Cadillac DTS is the basis for the car, even though it does not carry a model designation anymore.

Wrong Turn 2: Dead End (2007)

Jonesy says he read about Amber going to West Point. She was a Marine, and not in the Army, which is what West Point is for.

DELIBERATE MISTAKES

Something definitely done deliberately (rather than by oversight), but which still results in a mistake. Rare.

3 Ninjas (1992)

During the sting attempt towards the beginning, Douglas confronts Snyder on the roof of the building. A helicopter rises up from nowhere without making any sound prior to that.

Alice in Wonderland (2010)

When Alice jumps on the dog and they start running, her dress and her hand-band suddenly changed side. Probably they mirrored the image, and instead of going left as directed, it felt more accurate to go right.

Any Which Way You Can (1980)

At the end fight scene, when they are in the barn one of the men falls crashes through the wall when they get hit, spilling the fight to the outside. Unless the barn's walls were made of cheap plywood, the wall would not have given away so easily. Obviously done for dramatic purposes.

Austin Powers: The Spy Who Shagged Me (1999)

When Austin and Felicity cross the street when they are shopping, you can see green hills behind them, very much like Hollywood and not 1969 London. (Deliberate reference to an earlier joke)

A Beautiful Mind (2001)

Winners of the Nobel prize don't give an acceptance speech - they usually give a lecture before the award is given, and then at the most say "thank you," or in Nash's case "money would be nicer".

Ben-Hur (1959)

During the chariot race, the chariots crash together but the arrangement of the horses make it impossible for them to actually collide. In some instances (particularly in an aerial shot as Ben Hur and Messala round the turn) it is obvious that they repositioned the shaft of the chariot to between the first and third horses instead of being in the centre between the second and third.

The Big Lebowski (1998)

When we are introduced to Jesus, during his slow motion roll, the camera cuts to the ball hitting the pins and then back to Jesus doing a celebratory dance. For some un-known reason, the film of the ball hitting a strike is actually back to front (see the posters above the lane are in mirror image to what they should be). Given that a bowling lane is perfectly symmetrical, if anyone's got an explanation, I'd love to hear it... [Jesus bowls with his right hand. If the scene was played the correct way, you would realize the shot of the ball rolling was done by a LEFT HANDED bowler...so obviously rather than re-shoot the scene with a right-handed bowler they reversed the shot. Voila. Still a mistake but there's why.] (00:25:26)

Cars (2006)

During the very last race, Lightning McQueen gets next to the green car, and the reflection of that green car's chrome "C" emblem is seen on Lightning McQueen's hood. However, the C is facing the right way. Since the C is placed on the green car in the correct direction, the reflection on Lighting McQueen should be a mirror image.

The monitor from inside Mack's trailer displays his whole face while talking to McQueen. There is no camera outside of Mack that can display him in that fashion.

Buena Vista

Chariots of Fire (1981)

When we first see Eric Lidell, it is 1920 and he has just returned from China to his homeland of Scotland. Eric would've been 18 years old in 1920. Ian Charleson, who was 31 at the time the film was made, looks his own age.

Contact (1997)

The slow rate of the radio telescopes at the VLA has been greatly increased for the movie. They are actually quite slow and make little to no noise.

Darkman (1990)

There is just too much movement and detail in the synthetic skin masks. Peyton lost a large portion of his face in the explosion, and cannot make much expression with his own face, but somehow he can make the masks move perfectly just like a real face.

Donnie Darko (2001)

In the shot near the end of the film where Donnie grabs the keys for the station wagon, you can see a Blockbuster Video member card in a cup. That card design wasn't used until the mid to late 1990's. This movie is set in 1988. Deliberate as it's a product placement, but still wrong. (01:37:10)

Dressed to Kill (1980)

Has there ever been a more obvious body double than the one used for Angie Dickinson in the shower scene? Not only does the top of every shot stop right at the collarbones, she is much taller than Dickinson, she has a much deeper tan and (of course) her breasts are much, much bigger.

Failure To Launch (2006)

At one point they use a Red Ryder BB gun (Yes, just like in A Christmas Story) and the guy says "You pumped it more than twice, didn't you" to his female counterpart when they shoot the bird. Red Ryder BB guns cannot be cocked/pumped more than once, due to the simple nature of the toy gun that it is.

Fled (1996)

Practically all movies incorporate the name of the movie within the dialog. However, they must remember the English language and tense agreement. On at least two occasions, Fishburne says "Come on Dodge, lets FLED." If they were so interested in incorporating the name within the script, they should have named the movie FLEE.

Forrest Gump (1994)

In the scene where Forrest is describing his heritage, the clip of KKK on horses is taken from The Birth of a Nation. In this clip, you can see tire tracks on the dirt road well before automobiles were supposed to be in existence. Robert Zemeckis decided to leave this mistake in to perfectly match the clip to the original movie.

Fury (2014)

"Fury" director David Ayer acknowledges that he committed a deliberate error by having the German Tiger tank blast the last Sherman in the column, tank doctrine being that the lead vehicle in a column gets blasted, then the last to stall the column, leaving the vehicles in between the dead vehicles easy pickings. Ayer said if the doctrine was followed in the film, Brad Pitt's tank would have been destroyed first and thus the film would end, roll credits.

The Game (1997)

Every time Nicholas enters his gate at home, it's daylight and then when he drives up to the house it is night. Either he has a 300 mile property or there is something else going on. It would appear that it is deliberate as it happens many times in the film. Symbolically, Nick is leaving the world as he appears with wealth and privilege (light) and entering the real van Orton world of solitude and sadness (dark). (00:09:00 - 00:09:55)

Ghost Ship (2002)

When the passengers are cut by the wire while dancing, some of the clothing on the torsos defies gravity. A man's coat tails and pants fall but a woman's dress stays put when nothing would have held it from falling from her lower half in the same way. (00:04:00 - 00:05:10)

Warner Bros. Pictures

Gladiator (2000)

When the chariot crashes through the gate we see an explosion coming from both sides of the gate. However there is no reasonable explanation why there would be an explosion, so this was probably done to make the scene look more dramatic. (01:22:55)

Groundhog Day (1993)

When Phil wakes up at 6 AM, it's already bright outside. At 6 AM in February, it would still be pitch-dark. This was done intentionally by the director for the sake of the viewer, but still makes no sense.

Labyrinth (1986)

When Sarah, et al are surrounded by the Goblins in Goblin City, the first cannon fires causing an explosion in front of some buildings, one of which has a hanging sign with scissors on it. Later, after the squatty Goblin says, "Hey! I just fired you!" another cannon fires causing an explosion, and the very same shot is shown, only the first one was flipped. (01:20:15 - 01:25:35)

The Lion King (1994)

Rafiki is supposed to be a mandrill, but mandrills do not have tails. In the extended version DVD, there is a commentary by an animator who specifically admits that he knew that mandrills don't have tails (at least not like the length that Rafiki sports throughout the movie), but he put one on him anyway to make him more monkey-like. (00:02:40)

Live and Let Die (1973)

In the scene where Bond and Kananga are fighting underwater, Bond shoves the bullet in Kananga's mouth. Then Kananga rises up and explodes. He explodes like a balloon, with not much blood at all.

The Lord of the Rings: The Return of the King (2003)

Just after Gandalf shouts offscreen, "Fight! Fight to the last man! Fight for your lives!" there is a flipped close-up of Gandalf turning, when he hears Pippin shout, "Gandalf!" and his sword is at his right side, the opposite of the norm. (00:23:25)

After Skully orders the catapults to release the decapitated heads, shots of the Gondorian soldiers are flipped, which is noticeable in close-ups of their legs - note the sword sheaths that hang at their right sides, instead of left. (01:59:50)

Some moments after Gandalf whacks Denethor, the wizard rides Shadowfax up the stairs and all the archers' quivers hang on their right, instead of left. Then, the wizard shouts, "Send the foul beast into the abyss!" in a close-up that is flipped - note Gandalf's cloak broach, which is backwards. Another following close-up of the wizard is also flipped. All done for direction continuity. (02:01:55)

When Gandalf and Pippin quickly ride to the aid of Faramir and his men, who flee the Orcs at Osgiliath, in the first close-up of Gandalf and the Halfling, the wizard's silver broach is noticeably backwards - the shot is flipped for direction continuity. (01:12:40)

After Aragorn is crowned king he greets Legolas and they place their hands on each other's shoulder. In the shot facing Aragorn when he starts to move toward Arwen, the semi profile seen on Legolas is not Orlando Bloom, but that of his double. In the previous shot facing Legolas, Aragorn and the Elf are the same height and eye level, but in the shot facing Aragorn, Legolas is considerably taller. (02:55:05)

The Lord of the Rings: The Two Towers (2002)

On the Wall of the Hornburg, in the close-up of Aragorn, he dramatically draws his sword with his left gloved hand. In the next close-up of Aragorn, when he yells, "Hold!" he raises his left hand with the ring on his index finger. In editing, they wanted to have the Elves on the left of the screen and Uruk-hai on the right, so they flipped the first shot. (01:02:45)

During the Warg attack, Aragorn is being dragged by the Warg and is heading for the cliff. In the very last wide shot of Aragorn, from behind his head, we see the hillside and riders behind the Warg, where they just came from. Next, we see a couple of shots of Gimli finishing off a Warg. In the next wide shot, the hillside including riders and bodies is the same one as earlier, only it's been flipped. (00:12:50)

First there's a shot of Saruman as he communicates with Sauron using the palantir, then a shot of Barad-dur. Next we see the Orcs at Orthanc pulling down trees and a shot of a tree falling into the cavern below. In FotR, just after Gandalf catches the moth atop Orthanc, we see a shot of a tree falling into the cavern down below. These are the exact same shot, only it's been flipped in this movie. (00:20:00)

In two scenes in particular, Legolas is letting loose his arrow with his left hand, because of shot flipping. When he kills the Warg approaching Gimli and when Legolas severs the rope, causing the tall ladder to collapse. The ladder shots of Legolas were put together later during editing, because Peter J. wanted an extra 'hero' shot of Legolas at Helm's Deep. They took the same shots of Legolas trying to take out the Berserker Uruk-hai and flipped it to specifically fit the later scene of the ladders going up. Commentary, extended DVD. (01:08:55 - 01:17:30)

Madagascar (2005)

When Alex, Marty, Gloria and Melman are talking together inside the boxes, Alex has three holes in his box allowing light in for him. Melman, Marty and Gloria have that too, but Gloria's box is lying *under* Alex's and Marty's, so it can't get as much light - but it does.

Dreamworks

Marie Antoinette (2006)

In the scene where Marie is trying on shoes, a pair of powder blue high top Converse sneakers can be seen next to her feet. It must have been done intentionally, but since there is no trace of modern apparel anywhere else in the film (the closest would be the mere mention of hot pink dress fabric but, as it's not shown, we don't know what exactly Marie calls "hot pink") these shoes (and the fabric) can't be considered part of a thematic element or artistic license. (00:55:35)

Mars Attacks! (1996)

At the end just before the president is killed he fixes his tie, but it keeps on getting fixed to messed, to fixed, etc. Deliberate homage to "A Few Good Men", but worth looking for nonetheless. (00:28:15)

Matilda (1996)

When the Trunchbull is drinking from the glass with the newt in it, you can easily see that she doesn't actually drink anything, as the water level stays exactly the same. Logical, as the newt is real, but it's still very obvious because she drinks for about 15 seconds. (00:46:55)

Mulan (1998)

During the movie, when Mulan is just a girl, you can see that her eyelashes extend beyond her eyes. When she is pretending to be a boy, her eyelashes are short (this makes perfect sense). But when she is in the medical tent her eyelashes are long even though she had no time to put on makeup. This is deliberate though, because without it she would have still looked like a boy, and just pulling her hair down wouldn't make her look any different (since that's how she looked in the pond). So they had to change her eyelashes to make her look more girlish.

Nacho Libre (2006)

Several of the matches Nacho loses, he should actually have won. In Mexican pro wrestling, it is illegal to rip another's mask off, and results in immediate disqualification. This happens twice to Nacho, both in the fight with the midgets and in the final against Ramses.

New York Minute (2004)

After they have the towels on the girls, find the "I Love NY" shirts. They're wearing white bras when they shouldn't have anything on, considering they just took a shower.

Ocean's Twelve (2004)

Laser beams are normally not visible, except for a small dot where they hit a surface. Even if made visible, using smoke or dust or special glasses, they are thin as threads. Obviously something more visual was needed for Toulour's dance act, hence the thick beams of light.

The Order (2003)

There is one scene in the movie where Heath Ledger reads a Latin sentence in a book. As he is translating the sentence, he goes over the words one by one with his finger. This would never be possible in a Latin sentence, because words in Latin are never in exactly the same order as in English. Words that actually belong together can be placed at opposite ends of a sentence.

Osmosis Jones (2001)

The 'NNN' news program shows a picture of some animal crackers in Frank's stomach. The problem is, they are still all in one piece and are pretty big. I don't think Frank would swallow them whole.

Pirates of the Caribbean: The Curse of the Black Pearl (2003)

As was admitted on the commentary, the angle of the moonlight in the stateroom, which has a deep overhang outside of the doors, was deliberately vastly exaggerated, to enhance the shots with Governor Swann battling with the disembodied skeletal arm. (01:56:25)

Buena Vista Pictures

When Will is staring at Jacoby, another pirate comes up from behind him and hits Will on the head with a solid silver candlestick. The sound it makes when hitting Will's head is a sharp clang, as if it hit another metal, not reverberation. Post production thought it sounded more dramatic and funnier than a thud. (00:35:25)

Throughout the entire film the metalic rasping 'ching' sound is unrealistically heard, even when drawing swords from something like leather holders. Some examples are, at the cave, Jack draws a sword hanging across the shoulder of one of the pirates, and throws it to Will, whose hands are bound. At Jack's hanging, just before Will throws his sword into the trap door to save Jack, Will draws his sword from the brown leather strap. This is obviously done for dramatic effect. (01:52:10 - 02:06:15)

Pitch Black (2000)

In Paris' death scene, he blows alcohol onto his torch that illuminates the creatures around him. However the area is still illuminated after the light from his torch has disappeared. (01:12:05)

Pulp Fiction (1994)

Both in the first scene and last scene of the movie, we see Yolanda and Ringo starting the robbery by jumping from their seat and start threatening the costumers. In the first scene, Yolanda says "And I'll execute every motherfucking last one of you." But in the last scene the line changes to "and I'll execute every one of you motherfuckers". (00:04:40 - 02:18:00)

Rocky IV (1985)

When Rocky cuts Drago during round two of their fight, the punch actually hits Drago on the chin. His eye would not cut from that impact.

Sky High (2005)

Mr. Medulla said that Will stepped on his foot when he was walking to his desk. If you look closely you can notice that he stepped over his foot instead of on it.

Skyfall (2012)

In the chase through the tube station, Bond and Silva both slide down between the escalators. On the London Underground this area has hard vertical signs at regular intervals, precisely to prevent people sliding down. (01:31:50)

MGM

Spaceballs (1987)

There is a shot of the huge Yogurt statue that is in slow motion. You can see that the smoke from the statue is rising slower than it normally would. This was obviously done to make the shot longer for Mel Brooks' voice over to fit.

The Spy Who Loved Me (1977)

As the Lotus drives off the pier and enters the water, the exposed underbody is that of a normal car. After it enters the sea the underbody we see is completely sealed, which it needs to be to allow the car to submerge.

Star Wars: Episode I - The Phantom Menace (1999)

When Jar Jar gets arrested in the Gungan city, in the second shot of Jar Jar and Obi-Wan, Obi-Wan and a part of the floor behind him are reversed. This can be seen, for example, because two of the red areas on the floor have switched positions, and Obi-Wan's braid and lightsabre are on the wrong side. (00:14:00)

The Time Machine (2002)

When Alexander is travelling to the future for the first time, it shows a speedy acceleration of the events around him. However, the planes that are seen flying by are moving at normal speeds, or at least speeds way too slow since they should be moving too fast to even see, since skyscrapers are being built in a matter of seconds.

Titanic (1997)

Even though the movie uses the correct number of rockets, the timing is awful. The last rocket was fired at 1:40 AM at the latest. In the movie, the last rocket is fired when the last boat to be lowered on the davits leaves (the one Rose gets, and jumps off of). This would make it 2:05 in James Cameron's Titanic time. It was probably changed to add more drama to that heart-throbbing scene... (02:18:30)

True Lies (1994)

In the scene where the bad guy is attached to the missile and fired, in the split second before it hits the helicopter you can see below it a building called SUN BANK, but the letters are backwards. A close look reveals the likely reason - to the right of the reversed building is one which looks just like the building to the LEFT of the Sun Bank building behind the harrier a few seconds earlier. Most likely they couldn't film the chopper from the right side because there was a building there (the one the camera flies through), so they filmed it from the other side (the same side they'd filmed the harrier from), catching the "Sun Bank" behind, then had to flip it to have everything facing the right way. (02:06:55)

True Lies
Letters reverse (and chopper switches with harrier)

20th Century Fox

Unleashed (2005)

This was probably done intentionally to make them more visible, but the bullet holes left in the stairwell wall by Bart's handgun while he is chasing Danny during the movie's climax look to be about the size of golf balls. Typical handgun calibers aside, just looking at the size of the clip he's loading into the gun and seeing how many rounds it holds, those rounds would have to be much smaller than the holes the bullets made.

Vantage Point (2008)

In the point of view of the Hispanic cop, he is being led away by a secret service (SS) guy when the cop hears an explosion, he punches the secret service man but before the SS guy can react, the second explosion goes off. In all the other points of view, the first explosion goes off and there is 30-40 seconds of a break before the second explosion goes off. (It's clear the director needed the cop to have the distraction of the first explosion to attempt to get away, but in order for the cop to escape he had the second explosion go off seconds after).

OTHER MISTAKES

Any other kind of mistake.

2001: A Space Odyssey (1968)

There is something drastically wrong with the design of the spherical 'Aries' moon shuttle. Some seats and many fixtures are 'upside down' relative to the up-down orientation of the shuttle itself, and we see loose food trays and equipment about the place as if this is routine. But - the shuttle is designed to land on the moon. What happens then? The moon has gravity, remember? There are going to be quite a few very disgruntled people dangling upside down like spiders, and there will be loose gear (and perhaps a stewardess or two) bouncing about all over the place. It is not a matter of stowing loose gear or lying flat on landing - some parts of the shuttle are upside down relative to others, which is why the stewardess has to do that famous 180 degree upside down walk. Whichever way you look at it the shuttle is going to encounter serious problems when it reaches a gravity well, which will occur whenever the engines are fired up, never mind landing on the moon.

Adventures in Babysitting (1987)

The way 'Sara'/'Sarah' is spelled differs from the movie credits and the tag on the bottom of her roller skate shown near the end of the movie. (01:35:35 - 01:37:30)

Behind Enemy Lines (2001)

When Stackhouse and Burnett are being chased by the SAM,

they pull to the right after deploying flares and you hear a voice on the radio say "Chaff, Chaff, Chaff". Chaff is a cartridge of small metal strips released as a countermeasure for radar guided missiles. These small strips add noise to the radar and clutters it up giving the pilot about 5 seconds to evade the missile. Throughout the scene, several indicators such as the flares and exploding fuel tanks suggest that they are fleeing from a Heat-seeking missile, not a radar guided one. To add to this, the voice on the radio wasn't that of Stackhouse or Burnett and was added for radio effect. (00:20:20)

Blade II (2002)

Towards the end of the film, after Snipes beats the crap out of a lot of vampires, Whistler throws Blade's sunglasses to him. They show him throw them in one shot, then in the next shot they show Snipes catching them. But look in the background at Whistler, he doesn't have the glasses, but is moving his arm like he is throwing them. The glasses must have been computer animated, and bad editing contributed to this mistake. (01:37:34)

Blade Runner (1982)

When Deckard visits the Tyrell Corporation, he prepares to test Rachel with the "VK" machine. He is shown putting his briefcase of the table and lifting the "VK" machine out and onto the table. If you look closely, the "VK" machine is already on the table and Harrison Ford is miming the lifting - there is nothing in his hands! (00:19:45)

Boomerang (1992)

During the scene where Markus and Jackie are making love for the first time, as she is straddled on top of him, you can see that she that she is wearing knickers (panties).

Bride of Chucky (1998)

When Tiff picks up Chucky to throw him into the crib, you can tell that the Chucky doll is inactive and not on or alive. (00:21:20)

In the beginning, when Tiffany has just had her soul put into the bride doll, she is reading the "Voodoo for Dummies" book and Chucky tells her that the page she is looking for is in Chapter Six, page 217. When she flips to it, the camera shows the top of the page before panning downwards. On the top of the page it very clearly says "Chapter Eleven". (00:31:45)

The Call (2013)

When Casey is in the car boot on the phone to Jordan, Jordan is asking her to describe what she sees in the boot of the car. Casey is naming the items she sees, paint cans, shovel etc. Jordan asks her to pour the paint out of the boot through the tail light hole. Jordan puts out a call to look out for a car with "WHITE paint pouring out the back," but Casey didn't tell her the colour of the paint.

D2: The Mighty Ducks (1994)

When Julie Gaffeny knocks the 2 Iceland players over, she is ejected from the game. But later, after Adam scores the goal, the Iceland player winds his stick up over his head and crushes him, yet he only gets a 2 minute minor penalty.

Dangerous Minds (1995)

When Michelle Pfieffer hands out menus for the restaurant in the class, they all read them out loud in English. Then when she takes Raul there, he says he can't read it because it's in French.

Darkman (1990)

When Durant uses his cigar cutter to cut off Eddie's fingers, no blood is shown squirting from his severed digits and no blood is seen on the cigar cutter. (00:05:15)

Near the end, when Julie is pushed off the building by the henchmen, her handcuffs get caught on some rods that where sticking out. But this is impossible, by the way she was falling (vertically) the rods would have made contact between her legs. No way her handcuffs could have been caught like that. And they were sticking out a good foot or two from where her body was.

Die Another Day (2002)

When Bond arrives in Cuba and walks past the children dancing in the foreground you can see a man leaning on a wall holding a fishing rod looking directly into the camera, following it from left to right. (00:29:50)

MGM Pictures

During the James Bond windsurfing scene as he was escaping the ice, his hair and suit are dry in what seems to be 50 foot waves. (01:30:30)

Die Another Day
Hair dry in huge waves

MGM Pictures

Die Hard (1988)

In the shot where we see all the terrorists (except Karl and Theo, who are upstairs) walking into the building from downstairs, they are about to walk through a doorway when the camera cuts out. Watch the terrorist on the left (he's the one who guards the door) - the way he's walking he's going to smack straight into the wall! The shot cuts a fraction of a second before he does, but that's not a remotely normal walk/position - it's clearly just because it makes for a cool looking shot. (00:18:15)

20th Century Fox

After Powell frantically radios in his distress call, other police cars converge on the street in front of Nakatomi Plaza, blocking off both sides of the street. But when McClane grapples down the building using the firehose, you can see traffic on the street below and none of them are police.

When Bruce is looking on the touch-screen computer to find out where his wife is, he touches the name GENNARO, but when it changes colour it also corrects the spelling of his wife's name to GENNERO. (00:09:25)

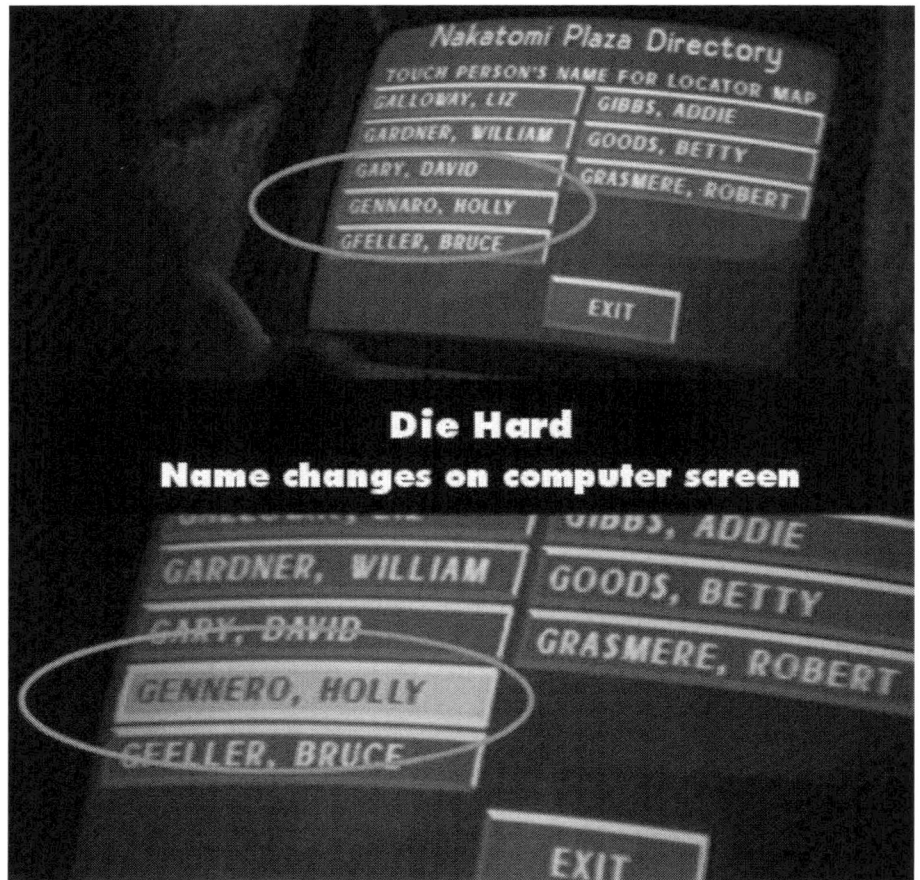

20th Century Fox

Friday the 13th Part 2 (1981)

Right at the part where Crazy Ralph is looking in on Paul and Ginny. Ralph hears a breaking of a stick behind him. You can see Jason put the barbed wire up and over the tree. How is that possible? He would have to whip it around the tree, not over it. (00:30:20)

From Russia With Love (1963)

When Tatiana enters Bond's room, he is about to take a shower. He never goes and turns it off. (00:51:10)

Frozen (2013)

Anna is shown from the front as she ascends an ice staircase inside Elsa's ice castle. There are giant ice pillars to Anna's right and left. They should reflect the side of her face, but instead the reflections show her face from the front.

Gangs of New York (2002)

Towards the end of the movie, when the mobs are breaking into stores/houses, the police come to try and stop them. The mob starts to throw rocks at the police. You can see one of these rocks, which look like they should be heavy, bounce right off of one of the officers' heads, and just bounce around as it hits the ground, like it weighs nothing at all. (02:14:30)

Garfield: The Movie (2004)

Jon's Volvo back license plate number in the first half of the movie is T03-851. When he and Dr Liz are looking for Odie, his front license plate number is I35-749. As they are pulling up to the train station, the Volvo in front of them also has the plate I35-749.

Garfield: The Movie
Two cars with same licence plate

20th Century Fox

The Goonies (1985)

When Andy plays the bone organ, the musical score on the back of the map clearly shows a melody consisting of single notes with only one or two chords. Still, Andy presses multiple keys on the organ to create chords EVERY time, not some single notes as the code shows. The code should not have worked if a person was playing only chords.

Halloween 4 (1988)

In the scene where Jamie is in the closet, looking at a photo of her mother (Jamie Lee Curtis). The photo looks exactly like the scene where Laurie is sitting waiting for Annie on the ledge in the original Halloween, which wasn't photographed at the time, it's clearly a still from the movie.

Halloween II (1981)

Watch the scene where the drunk Ben Tramer (wearing a similar

Michael Myers mask) was hit by the speeding cop car and then pinned against the parked van before burning. Even taking out the equation of accidentally hitting Ben Tramer, what was the cop car doing speeding at that rate of speed, head on towards a parked van on a side street? Remember, we only hear screeching brakes AFTER the car hits Tramer, and we never see the cop car swerve or any of that to miss hitting the van. Seems that even if Tramer hadn't been there, the cop car was sure to barge head on right into that van.

Harley Davidson and the Marlboro Man (1991)

There is a patch on the jacket Harley (Rourke) wears, that appears and disappears throughout the movie. It's on the front lower right side. It is there when he's standing outside their friends' bar with Marlboro, it's gone when they are inside.

Hellfighters (1968)

The crew goes up to Calgary in January to extinguish an oil fire, yet there's no snow on the ground, the grass is green, and all the deciduous trees have leaves.

The Hunger Games: Catching Fire (2013)

The old man executed in District 11 was shot in the head from behind. However, when Katniss looks out the window from above there are no blood stains on the floor, nor is there a gunshot wound to the head. (00:20:50 - 00:22:30)

While Katniss and Johanna are unreeling the wire on the way to the beach, it snags (or is deliberately pulled) behind a rock and Katniss tugs on it till it snaps. The wire was coming off a spool and becoming caught up would have no effect on how the wire unreeled, because the spool would keep on turning regardless. In fact, a taut wire behind her would be what she wanted. (02:05:35)

Into the Storm (2014)

When the blue van rolls over, and they turn around to go pick them up, they park like 20-30 feet from the van for no reason, instead of right by it, seemingly just to have a tree block their path, then decide to run into a church with really big stained glass window and wood pews while a fire tornado is just outside. Rolling the van back upright, all the TVs and equipment inside the van seem to be working just fine.

Into the Wild (2007)

The closing captions state that Chris McCandless' sister Carine flew "his" brother's ashes home, instead of "her" brother's ashes.

It's a Wonderful Life (1946)

Clarence tells George that his brother died at the age of 9 because he wasn't there to save him from falling through the ice, but when you see the tomb stone, it shows Harry Bailey was born in 1911 and died in 1919. That would make Harry only 7 or 8 years old.

Juice (1992)

In the scene following the robbery, the four young men, led by Tupac Shakur and Omar Epps, run into a brick court, walled on four sides. Shakur states he's going to keep the gun, despite suggestions that they ditch it. He has a revolver stuck in his jeans, by his left hip. When he is challenged about keeping the gun, he pulls another revolver from his pocket, scuffles with one of his friends and shoots him in the chest - all the while the grip of the other identical revolver is in view.

The Last Airbender (2010)

Before the battle, the leader of the waterbenders says that he will have everyone extinguish as many sources of fire as possible. When the firebenders come up from the ground at the start of the battle, all of the torches lighting the city are lit.

The Little Rascals (1994)

When Alfalfa takes some flowers to Darla, Waldo (the rich boy) turns up and Darla's friends comment on the rich kid. As one girl is saying her line, 'He's smoother than a baby's bottom' you can see the girl next to her mouthing the same line.

The Martian (2015)

During the storm scene in the beginning of the movie, the astronauts' faces inside the helmets are brightly lit, meaning there's a light source pointed directly in their face. That's something that would render them mostly blind and unable to see and appears to be nothing but a dramatic effect for the camera. (00:05:00 - 00:08:00)

When devising the plan to retrieve Watney, it is mentioned that the Hermes crew have had to lash together all the webbing on board to make the longest possible tether. When this tether is used, there is no evidence of any lashing together or other extensions or modifications to lengthen it. The tether is one continuous length and is stored on a reel that was designed for the length of tether gathered on it.

The Natural (1984)

In the top of the ninth inning of the game against the Cubs, both the scoreboard and the radio announcer state that the score is 4-3 in favor of the Cubs. However, when Hobbs is at bat, the radio announcer says "Blevins is at 3rd base, 3 to 3". (01:14:00)

The One (2001)

In the penal scene with the pyramid, Yulaw knocks a person off the pyramid, and he rolls down the steps. A short way down, he stops rolling, and you can see him push himself off another step to get himself rolling again. (01:16:40)

The Package (1989)

Sergeant Johnny Gallagher (Gene Hackman) and Lieutenant Milon Delich (Dennis Franz) are in a supposedly deserted building searching for a group of conspirators who plan to assassinate both the USA and USSR presidents. Delich finds a police colleague of his in the building, and Delich kills his colleague. When he fires his revolver, the sound of the blanks can be heard, slightly out of synch with the gun blasts on the sound track.

Panic Room (2002)

Near the end of the movie Dwight Yoakam is holding Jodie Foster's daughter captive as he tries to exit the house. Jodie Foster sneaks up behind him with a sledgehammer and swings it at his head. He turns to face her and the metal end of the hammer catches him firmly in his temple, knocking him down a flight of stairs. A few minutes later he comes up the stairs and tackles Jodie Foster to the ground, seemingly unhurt by the impact of the sledgehammer.

Paul Blart: Mall Cop (2009)

When Paul Blart is pwning Rock Band, the vocals shows the tambourine/clap notes. Paul Blart is doing nothing that would play those notes (singing or pressing the "a" button).

Practical Magic (1998)

In the end credits, the filmmakers misspell the name of the town they wish to thank. They spell it "Coupville", but it's actually spelled "Coupeville."

A Quiet Place (2018)

The construction of a staircase does not require a large nail at the site shown on the steps. Furthermore when Emily snags her clothes basket on the stairs it lifts a small nail up. How did it grow into a 2 inch fat nail?

Resident Evil: Afterlife (2010)

Wesker's chamber on the Arcadia has only one entrance, a big blast door which Alice walks through. Yet Chris and Claire manage to appear behind Wesker without the blast door ever being opened.

Rocky III (1982)

At the beginning of the scene when Rocky's statue is unveiled and Clubber Lang challenges Rocky to a fight, the camera zooms out of one of the drums that is being played and it is easy to spot that Mr. T's signature is scrawled right across the centre of the drum.

Snow White and the Seven Dwarfs (1937)

When the Dwarfs first leave the mine entrance, the first few animation cells seem to have been omitted, so that at first the entrance is empty and then the Dwarfs appear out of thin air.

Snow White and the Seven Dwarfs
Dwarfs instantly appear in the same shot

Buena Vista

Star Trek IV: The Voyage Home (1986)

After they take off from California, Kirk gives a heading to Alaska. He then tells Sulu "full impulse power", and Sulu says "aye, ETA 12 minutes." Full impulse is 1/4 the speed of light. No way they would use speeds like that to go a few thousand miles.

Star Wars (1977)

In the first shot of the Millennium Falcon in the special edition, the top of the ship is missing its radar dish. (00:54:30)

20th Century Fox

Subtitling and translation can also lead to weird mistakes. Han Solo says (twice in the special edition) that he dumped his cargo because "Even I get boarded sometimes", and in Dutch cinemas the subtitles read as if he said "Even I get bored sometimes." (00:50:35 - 00:53:25)

Star Wars: Episode V - The Empire Strikes Back (1980)

When the Falcon gets hit by an asteroid, Leia falls and is caught by Han. She tells him that "being held by you isn't quite enough to get me excited". As she is saying this you can clearly see Harrison Ford mouthing her exact words. (00:44:05)

Star Wars: The Clone Wars (2008)

During the Battle of Teth (the pillared jungle planet), the AT-TE's shoot the ledge at the top and there's not a single mark on the ledge afterwards, despite being hit with several joules worth of fire.

Swimfan (2002)

When Madison is giving a cello concert at her house, there is vibrato in the music that she doesn't do while playing. In the music, there are low notes on the C and G strings, but she only fingers on the A string, and sometimes she forgets to move the bow while playing.

The Tailor of Panama (2001)

In the scene where Geoffrey Rush is folding his dead friend's hands, you can see the dead man's fingers scratching to accommodate the final resting place of his hands. (01:30:45)

Thor (2011)

On one of the SHIELD monitors, "perimeter" is spelled

"perimiter".

Tooth Fairy (2010)

In a hockey game, Derek Thompson slams an opposing player into the wall and knocks out a tooth. Inexplicably, the tooth shoots straight up into the air and there is absolutely no blood on the tooth or around the player's mouth.

Toy Story 2 (1999)

When Hamm turns off the TV at the beginning, there's no reflection of him, Rex who is beside him, or the remote. (00:06:58)

Toy Story 2
No reflection of TV watchers

Jon Sandys

Buena Vista Pictures

Transformers: Dark of the Moon (2011)

So let me get this straight: Optimus Prime has Energon Swords hidden in both of his arms, with which he can slice through an entire Decepticon in one chop, yet when he is hanging from a few wires, despite having one arm entirely free, he can't cut himself loose?

Twister (1996)

Although the film is set in Oklahoma (and north of Oklahoma City), the roads are marked by Texas road signs.

THE END

Thank you for reading! I hope you enjoyed it, and if so please tell your friends, share it, lend it...spread the word! Please leave a review on Amazon - if you like this, there's plenty more where this came from. And if you've got any observations of your own, please submit them to moviemistakes.com. I'd love to hear any suggestions, corrections, thoughts and opinions - please get in touch at jon@moviemistakes.com.

More books

Great Movie Mistakes

Great Movie Mistakes 2

Great Movie Trivia

Great TV Mistakes

Great TV Mistakes 2

Printed in Poland
by Amazon Fulfillment
Poland Sp. z o.o., Wrocław